My Best Wishes —
Betty
Tufts

Tales of North Berwick

Or You Can't Get There From Here

by

Betty Kennedy Tufts

Bloomington, IN — Milton Keynes, UK

AuthorHouse™
1663 Liberty Drive, Suite 200
Bloomington, IN 47403
www.authorhouse.com
Phone: 1-800-839-8640

AuthorHouse™ UK Ltd.
500 Avebury Boulevard
Central Milton Keynes, MK9 2BE
www.authorhouse.co.uk
Phone: 08001974150

© 2006 Betty Kennedy Tufts. All rights reserved.

No part of this book may be reproduced, stored in a retrieval system, or transmitted by any means without the written permission of the author.

First published by AuthorHouse 8/21/2006

ISBN: 1-4259-3686-5 (sc)

Printed in the United States of America
Bloomington, Indiana

This book is printed on acid-free paper.

Dedication

This is for my mother and dad

Sarah George Kennedy

and

Thomas Francis Kennedy

With thanks to them

for so much.

A Special Thanks

The <u>Drawings</u> are by Nathaniel Tufts Parry with thanks from his grandmother.

About the Recipes

A few were collected from <u>The State of Maine Rebekah Cookbook</u> 1935. <u>York County Cook Book</u> published by York County WCTU in 1941.

And a few gems are from <u>Non-Pareil Cook Book by the Ladies of North Berwick, ME</u> 1889

Mrs. Harriett Littlefield, whose recipes were published therein, passed on her cookbook to her granddaughter, Sue Littlefield Stillings who shared them with me. I have included several in this collection.

Most all the recipes are from family and friends along the way.

Contents

Dedication v
A Special Thanks.. vii
About the Recipes ix
The Town.. 1
This is How It Started................................... 2
Ginnie's Oatmeal Bread................................ 5
Mary Hurd and Me....................................... 6
Spiced Cookies.. 9
That Footstool was Ugly............................. 10
Show Off Rhubarb Pie................................ *13*
The Congregational Church....................... 14
Annie Neal's Molasses Cookies.................. 19
Cocoa For 50.. 20
Bean Suppers.. 21
Cranberry – Raspberry Salad..................... *24*
Baked Beans... *25*
One Lump or Two...................................... 27
Strawberries.. 30
Pink Ladies (Bars)...................................... 31
Kid Stuff... 32
Divinity Fudge... 38
Corn Balls.. 39
Long Johns and Beach Pajamas................. 40
Chocolate Cake.. 43
Molded Tomato Aspic............................... 44

How I Gave Up Smoking at Age 9... 45
Twenty Minute Pound Cake..................... 47
A Passenger for Mr. Sundstrom... 48
Swedish Tea Ring...................................... *50*
Swedish Meatballs... 52
Merry-go-round... 53
Frozen Custard.. 56
Beneath the Sea Salad................................ 57
The Village Smithy... 58
Baked Rice Pudding.................................. 60
Hearty Pressure Cooker Stew... 61
Sixteen Polliwogs....................................... 62
Cape Cod Pot Roast................................... 64
Corn Pudding... 65
School's Out... 66
Aggression Cookies... 69
Pickled Eggs... 70
High School Came Next... 71
Grapenut Pudding..................................... 74
Tingie Mows Down a Heifer..................... 75
Marion Littlefield's Baked Turnip.............. *77*
Remember Prize Speaking... 78
Graham Cracker Pudding... 81
Tales Out of School.................................... 82
Oven Barbecued Spare Ribs... 87
The 1940 Jct Set... .... *88*
Scalloped Oysters... 91
Crab Cakes in Washington D.C................. 92

I Had the Itch…	93
Barbecued Hot Dogs…	96
Poor Quasimodo…	97
Margaret's Rigatoni…	99
Gallia Est…	100
Chocolate Crinkle Cookies…	102
Big Doings in Commercial Hall…	103
Blueberry Pancakes…	109
The Brits…	110
Yorkshire Pudding…	112
North Berwick Puts on the Dog…	113
Calico Beans…	117
Sure Cures…	118
Clam Fritters…	123
Old Crow…	124
Spaghetti and Meat Balls…	126
We Made Our Own Root Beer…	127
Cheese Cake…	129
Mel Learns to Drive	130
Afternoon Tea Doughnuts…	132
We'll Ride Up to Dover…	133
Beef Casserole…	136
Crochet, Knit, and Embroider…	137
Dumplings…	140
Mason Jars and Vinegar…	141
Potsfield Pickles…	144
Mustard Pickles…	145
Tripping the Light Fantastic…	146

Sweet 'n' Sour Meatballs... ... 148
Spring Cleaning... ... 149
Cornflake Pudding... ...152
And Then There Were These... ...153
Apple Cake... ...157
The Corset Lady... ...158
Red Cinnamon Apple Pie... ... 160
A Bell for Our Town... ...161
Ruth Stillings' Baking Powder Biscuits... ... 163
Shave and a Hair Cut... ... 164
Orange Sponge Cake... ... 169
The Hair Bob and Nail Polish... ... 170
Baked Rice Pudding... ... 173
Food Sales and Cookbooks... ...174
Brambles... ... 177
The Pharmacist and The Soda Man... ... 178
The Perfect Hand Lotion... ...181
Boyle Brothers Store... ... 182
Don't Worry's Hermits... ... 185
Parcel Post or RFD... ... 187
Walnut Strips... ... 190
Ice Cream and Fireworks... ...191
Norwegian Apple Pie... ... 194
Norwegian Macaroons... ... 195
The Great Atlantic and Pacific 196
Favorite Ginger Snaps... ... 198
J.O. MacCorison, Mr. North Berwick... ... 199
Maine Shrimp Casserole... ... 201

Cherry Cake... 202
North Berwick and the B & M............... 203
Salmon Loaf... 207
Current Events.. 208
Mushroom Sandwich............................. 213
Downeast Blueberry Cobbler..................214
Hillside...215
Banana Bread..219
Maine Talk.. 220
Household Hints from a 1930s
Cookbook... 222

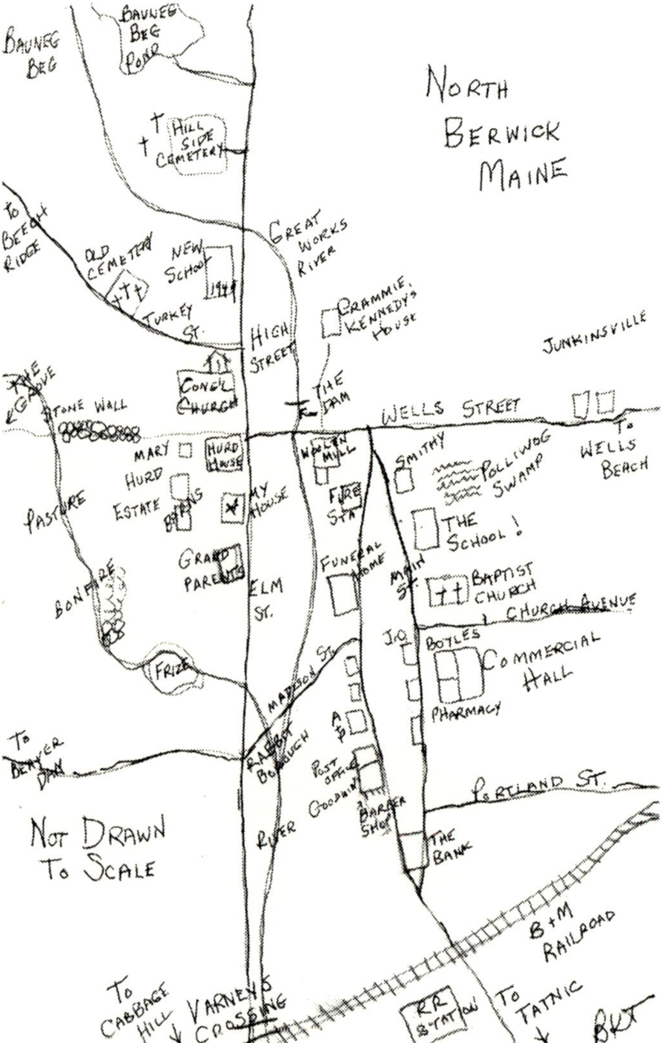

NORTH BERWICK MAINE
BAUNEG BEG
BAUNEG BEG POND
HILL SIDE CEMETERY
TO BEECH RIDGE
OLD CEMETERY
NEW SCHOOL
1949
TURKEY ST.
GREAT WORKS RIVER
GRAMMIE KENNEDY'S HOUSE
HIGH STREET
JUNKINSVILLE
THE GROVE
CONG'L CHURCH
THE DAM
STONE WALL
WELLS STREET
TO WELLS BEACH
MARY HURD ESTATE
HURD HOUSE
WOOLEN MILL
SMITHY
POLLIWOG SWAMP
PASTURE
BARNS
MY HOUSE
FIRE STA
THE SCHOOL!
GRAND PARENTS
FUNERAL HOME
MAIN ST.
BAPTIST CHURCH
CHURCH AVENUE
BONFIRE
ELM ST.
J.O.
BOYLES
COMMERCIAL HALL
MADISON ST.
PHARMACY
TO BEAVER DAM
POST OFFICE
GOODWIN
BARBER SHOP
PORTLAND ST.
NOT DRAWN TO SCALE
RIVER
THE BANK
B+M RAILROAD
TO CABBAGE HILL
VARNEY'S CROSSING
RR STATION
TO TATNIC
BKT

The Town...

North Berwick is a small town in York County, southernmost in the state of Maine, about ten miles from the coast. The land is gently hilly with Bauneg Beg Hill on the northern end looking to the ocean on a clear day.

North Berwick has several well named areas: Tatnic, Beech Ridge, Rooster Hill, Rabbitborough, Junkinsville, Bauneg Beg, Beaver Dam, Cabbage Hill and Turkey Street. You have to be a native to know where you are. North Berwick, as I knew it was like a big neighborhood made up of real people sharing their lives. They truly cared for one another and enjoyed the closeness.

These are stories of the people in the town before 1950. As far as I know, these stories are all true, mostly from my life and a few from family members. The recipes are from old books, old cooks and old times.

It is important to me to remember them all.

This is How It Started…

My great grandfather, Thomas Kennedy, emigrated from Ireland in 1850. On the stormy Atlantic crossing to America, he fell in love with a little Irish girl, Ann Kenney, on her way to a new country. After they landed, both nineteen years old, they married and went to Providence, Rhode Island to look for work. One day, young Tom found a wallet on the street and he took it to the police station. It belonged to Friend William Hill, a Quaker, from North Berwick, Maine, who was in Providence for a yearly meeting of the Quakers.

When Friend Hill looked up young Thomas to thank him, he said he had found an honest man and offered Tom a job on the spot as herdsman on his farm in North Berwick. Friend Hill also owned the woolen mill and much land in town. Grandfather took the job and he and Ann settled in North Berwick in the house in the lane beside the river and dam. They lived there the rest of their lives.

Young Tom was well regarded by the Hill family and later on by the Hurds. Mary Hurd, Friend Hill's daughter, had taken over the farm and the mill. Mary Hurd showed me the glass photograph of my great grandfather that she kept on a chain in the window.

Much later, Tom and Ann's son Herbert and my grandmother Lizzie moved to the house down the lane and next to them. As grandparents, they were overjoyed. Here were six grandchildren for them. This little Irish woman, with a kerchief tied around her head, half covering her red hair, would time her bread to come out of the oven just before school let out each day. This way she could have hot bread and molasses for the children on their way home from school. The children liked to go into the woods with her when she gathered herbs for home remedies. Their use is now long gone.

Another advantage for these grand-parents was to see to the religion of the six grandchildren. Most Sundays Grandfather Kennedy hitched up his team and took the kids to the Catholic Church in South Berwick, since there was no Catholic Church in North Berwick. On the other side of the story, when the children stayed in Portsmouth with the Treadwell grandparents, they went to the Protestant church; the Unitarian, I believe.

All this religious training paid off for my father when he was stationed at the naval base in Newport, Rhode Island during the first World War. Once in a while, the Chaplain would pass on an invitation for a couple of Catholic sailors to attend mass with the family and share their Sunday dinner. Dad went. He could be right at home with those Catholics. And then when a Protestant family wanted a couple of Protestant sailors for church, and a pot roast dinner, Dad could do that too. He was prepared to go either way, thanks to his grandparents.

Ginnie's Oatmeal Bread…

Cook until thick but moist
1 cup oatmeal
2 cups boiling water

Cool

Add…
½ cup molasses
1 tablespoon salt
3 tablespoons butter

When cool add…
1 yeast cake dissolved in ½ cup lukewarm water

Stir in…
6 cups flour approximately

Raise double size.

Stir down and let rise again.

Put in pans to rise again.
Bake for 1 hour in a 350-degree oven.

I have made this bread for 50 years.

Mary Hurd and Me...

Mary Hurd's biography may be written about her business acumen, her toughness in financial deals, and her ever interest in North Berwick. She was the daughter of Friend William Hill, the Quaker who brought the woolen cloth manufacturing business to North Berwick. She inherited the mill and its assets and took a very active role in taking care of it all. I knew her as the elderly lady next door, who owned all the barns, animals, and pastures in back of our house. I remember her as an interesting small lady with frizzy gray hair and gold teeth. She wore long black dresses with white lace collars, She used her cane as a weapon when she appeared on her front veranda and yelled at the kids to get off her iron fence.

During the town centennial celebration parade in 1931, she asked me to ride on the North

Berwick Woolen Mill float on Mack Littlefield's truck with a live lamb. I dressed as Little Bo-Peep, wearing a pretty pink outfit – dress, hat and pantaloons – which Mrs. Hurd and her daughter, Miss Margaret, had rented from Boston. I sang two solos in an evening performance before the Staples Brothers Quartet sang. E.P. Spinney, our town judge, was Master of Ceremonies.

Afterward, I was summoned now and then to The House to sing for the two elderly ladies. My mother copied the rented pink outfit and made me a blue one of my own. Wonderful refreshments were always served at those command performances.

Mrs. Hurd, next door, owned our house. It had belonged to Friend Hill, her father, and was her childhood home. She kept the old house in perfect order and was pleased that my mom and dad were proud of it. When I was 10 or 11, I knew that repairs came by the way of Mrs. Hurd. One day, I went on my own to ask if I could have my bedroom papered and painted. (My parents were not happy with me when they found out.) Mrs. Hurd promised me that she would send Billy Varney to do the work after I picked out wallpaper that I liked. And she did.

Behind the mansion and our house was a carriage house, two huge barns of cows, Belgian workhorses and wonderful painted farm vehicles. Day Benway and Granville Littlefield ran the farm. They let Albion Lane, Barbara Kezar and I feed the cattle and ride on the wagons. We spent many hours roaming the place. We loved it. One day when Barbara and I were playing on the stonewall in the pasture – probably arranging it to our liking – we were terrified to discover there were 14 big steers in the same pasture with us. Trapped! We waited hours for those steers to drift down to the river and away. We didn't do that again.

Mrs. Hurd and the North Berwick Woolen Company owned 20 houses in our town. She had her chauffeur, Len Bracy, drive her all over town in her big black Packard to check on her property. If any place needed painting or cleaning she had it done and strongly ordered the tenants to keep things up.

Mary Hurd was a true benefactor and North Berwick never looked so good and thriving as it did in her day. I wonder what she would think of our town today.

Spiced Cookies...

1 cup molasses
1 cup sugar
1 cup milk
2 eggs
1 teaspoon cinnamon
1 teaspoon cloves
1 teaspoon nutmeg
1 teaspoon soda

Enough flour to mix rather soft

Bake in roll pan

1 cup of raisins is an improvement.

Mrs. Mary R. Hobbs
(Mary Hurd)
Non Pariel Cookbook
1889

This is the only recipe I have ever seen contributed by Mary Hurd. This is written exactly as it came out in the 1889 cookbook.

That Footstool was Ugly...

In the 1930s when I was a 4th or 5th grader, I often stopped by to see my Grammie Kennedy who lived at the end of the lane beside the river. It was a ritual for us. Grammie would ask me what I had learned in school that day. My answer was always the same, "Nothing." And we all laughed…every time. By that time, Aunt Florence had given me a lunch. I loved that tapioca pudding with the floating meringue on top.

Aunt Florence and I talked about all of the antiques in the house. To begin with, my grandmother had been the only daughter of a Portsmouth, New Hampshire cabinetmaker and most of Grammie's antiques were made by her father. There were all kinds of interesting things to look over. There was a doll's buggy with wooden wheels and fancy reed scrolls on the sides. There was the Victorian sofa with the rose carvings along the top and upholstery in black shiny horsehair that made the back of my leg itch. "The Old General" was the grandfather clock with the wooden gears that kept perfect time.

Many times I looked over the Victorian footstool with bamboo legs. It had a round top covered with carpeting and bound all around with ball fringe that was sadly missing half of the balls. That footstool was pretty ugly. Even a nine year old knew that! Hoping to make it at least interesting, if not pretty, I wrote underneath the top in my best handwriting, "This footstool came over on the Mayflower." Quite an exaggeration, but I felt that now that stool had something going for it.

When Grammie died in 1935, all of her antiques went to Aunt Florence. Then in 1972, they went on to Aunt Ethel in Sanford. Eventually, many of her wonderful old things came to me in 1982. By that time I had my own antiques shop on US Route 1 in Wells. I kept everything from my grandmother's house except that ugly footstool. I sold that for $16 to another antiques dealer in New Hampshire. I figured that was the last of it. Not so.

In 1996, I stopped at an antiques shop on the Coast of Maine in Searsport. I could not believe my eyes when I saw *that* footstool featured in a display, sitting proudly on a shelf. There it was. I was sure it was the same one that my great grandfather had made in Portsmouth, New Hampshire in the 1880s. I turned over the stool. Yup. There it was, written in a childish hand, "This footstool came over on the Mayflower." The price was $127. Do you suppose that someone believed that or even laughed about it? I didn't buy it. I left it. It was ugly!

Show Off Rhubarb Pie...

2 eggs well beaten
¾ cup sugar
¼ cup flour
¼ teaspoon of salt

Mix together
Add 4 cups of sliced rhubarb - mix well
Arrange in pie shell and dot with butter.
Top with criss-cross pastry strips

Bake at 450 degrees for 15 minutes
Reduce heat to 350 degrees for 30 minutes more

Alice Wyman

The Congregational Church...

In my childhood, there were 2 churches in town: the Baptist and the Congregational. Most families in town belonged to one or the other, and I went to the Congregational. We all went to Sunday School every Sunday, patent leather shoes and all. First, when we were very young, we had Margaret Hobbs and Elizabeth Guptill for teachers. They were kind and so dedicated to children. We sat in small chairs and sang songs. We all had little cardboard banks for pennies for the children somewhere that were poor. All the way up through the grades, we had good people who taught us the Bible and listened to us sing.

On the top of this Victorian church was the tall steeple and the big bell. Somehow every kid worth his salt got to climb those narrow stairs up to the belfry to scare those innocent pigeons that were just there hanging out and laying eggs. There was a wonderful view of the whole town and we were the kings of the hill.

In the past the ministers were Mr. Getchell, Earl Osborne, Mr. Dubbs and Mr. Kirchbaum. It was Mr. Osborne who served as minister in my time. He was a deep thinker with a strong conscience for racial equality. I think he was the first who talked to us about the problems of the Races. North Berwick was a little town in New England and most of us had never known a black person. Mr. Osborne's sermons were rousing and gave us a new dimension in our thinking.

Mr. Osborne turned out to be a forgiving soul when I broke the wooden collection plate. This is how it happened. The church was never locked. One summer day the three of us, Christine Welch, Natalie Kennedy and I, decided to see what it was like to run a church service. It seemed like a good idea at the time. Christine made believe she was playing the organ. Natalie was in the pulpit holding forth on a sermon and was just getting warmed up. I was swinging down the aisle wildly with the collection plate, and smashed off one whole side of the plate on the back of an oak pew. I was horrified. My friends took off, which was no help to me. So I ran home and told my mother what I had done. It didn't take her very long to send me right back to the minister and confess. Wow! Did I drag my feet. Mr. Osborne was very calm when he listened to me and then he said we'd have to fix it. We used gobs of glue to fit that plate back together, and not a neat job either. I was so grateful to him. I had thought I'd be excommunicated from the church. But I must say, that plate dogged my footsteps ever after. Every time I went to church, that plate always found its way down my side of the aisle.

There were several groups in the church. The oldest ladies group was the Willing Workers who also were the oldest in age. They were always busy doing all kinds of good stuff. Some of them were Ruby Grant, Carrie Shaw, Ethel Austin, Pearl Lincoln, and Lydia Johnson, and there were a few others as well. One time my mother fixed a dress for Lydia. As she worked on it she realized the figures on the print dress fabric were all cigarettes with make believe smoke. Lydia, 75 years old, had not known what the figures were on her new dress until my mother told her. Poor Lydia was embarrassed at first and then she thought it was a good joke. After that when she wore the dress to church, Lydia, who had never smoked a cigarette in her life, held a pencil in her hand and furtively made believe puffing and smoking for my benefit. No one knew but me. She and I had a good laugh every time.

Every summer there was Vacation Bible School and the PASTE! Every kid got a daub of it in a little tin plate. It smelled so good, we all had to taste it. It was awful stuff. We pasted pictures, sewed yarn, glued paper chains and carved Palestine flat roofed houses out of cakes of Ivory soap. Whatever good those crude carvings of soap were, escaped me. Seemed like a waste of good soap. John Chadbourne had us making lopsided clay pots. They weren't too bad when we found out what they were supposed to be. All week we sang songs and learned Bible verses and on Friday night, our parents came to see all that we had done.

Then there was summer camp. Every year our state Congregational Church took over a young peoples' camp and for one week, teenagers from all over the state attended Camp Manitou (the Indian word for God.) One year my cousin Natalie Kennedy, Roscoe Littlefield and I went there. Mr. Osborne, our minister and Mr. Getchell (a retired minister who must have been ninety at the time but came along for the ride) drove us down to the camp in Washington, Maine. They saw that we were lodged in safely. The bad side of that was the fact that the two preachers ate almost all of my chocolate cookies that my mother had made for Nat and me to see us through the week. I was generous to offer them my cookies. Mistake! They were hooked on my mother's cooking and the ride was long, so the cookies were gobbled up before we even hit our destination.

Nat and I made quite a splash at Camp Manitou. It was 1935 or 1936 that Joseph P. Kennedy (father of Jack, Ted and Bobby and 6 others) became the United States Ambassador to Great Britain at the Court of St. James. It was just too good to miss. With a last name of Kennedy, Natalie told everyone at that camp that we were nieces of old Joseph P. She said that we were planning a trip later on in the summer to visit "our" uncle Joe and his family in London. This was about the time Edward VIII quit being King of England and that made it sound pretty exciting. She had everyone taken in by this. Natalie was good at that. She was never backward about coming forward. She could dream up great stuff. She and I had a week's worth of fame.

Whether it was caroling at Christmas, cantatas at Easter, harvest suppers in the fall, or a steady devotion to the church, our Congregational Church was a pillar of strength in our town.

Annie Neal's Molasses Cookies...

2 cups molasses
½ cup sugar
1 cup shortening
1 teaspoon salt
2 teaspoons ginger
1 teaspoon cinnamon
½ cup sour milk
2 teaspoons soda
5-6 cups flour

Dissolve soda in milk.
Blend in rest of ingredients
Refrigerate 3-4 hours
Roll out and cut in shapes
Bake 350 degrees for 10 minutes.

Annie Neal
1889
Mrs. Neal had three sons: Lloyd, Vinton and Ronnie, and I am sure she made lots of these cookies. Mrs. Neal was a Sunday school teacher for a long time.

Betty Kennedy Tufts

Cocoa For 50...

1 ½ cups cocoa
1 quart cold water
2 quarts of boiling water
6 quarts scaled milk
¾ quart sugar
2 teaspoons salt

Mix cocoa with cold water
Add boiling water
Boil for 5 minutes
Add remaining ingredients

We always had cocoa after Caroling at Christmas
1935

Bean Suppers...

All winter long, Saturday night public bean suppers were very popular. They were great moneymakers for the church or the Masons or the Pocahontas ladies. Maybe you don't know about the Pocahontas. The women were the female counterparts of the Red Men, a popular lodge then. What they did or what they wore was a mystery to anyone who wasn't one. My mother-in-law never missed a Wednesday night meeting even if her entire family was coming to Thanksgiving dinner the next day. She carried a black case when she went to a meeting and her sons teased her about what was in the box. Was it a fringed sash? Was it a make believe deerskin dress? No matter what it was, that getup would probably insult the Indians.

Back to the beans. First you had to find someone who could bake the beans, twenty pounds of kidney and twenty pounds of pea beans. The bean baker (having put the beans in to soak the night before) was committed all day to keeping those beans stirred and moving and watered, after all the spices and molasses and brown sugar had been put together with a sizable slab of salt pork and three or four gallons of water. Those beans were the main event of the suppers. They had to be just right to serve to a bunch of bean experts who had been eating baked beans every Saturday night their whole lives. Beans mushy? No. Hard as marbles? No. Like in *Goldilocks and the Three Bears*, the beans had to be just right. Potato salad, cole slaw, hot dogs or ham, pie, rolls and coffee went along with the main event....**the Beans.**

The pie cutter was the Prima Donna of the kitchen. First she had to cut the pie in even portions. There was always a big row whether to cut six or seven slabs out of one pie. Next she had to hold the runny pies together while being tactful about it. Sometimes she kept whipped cream at the ready for a little touch up. When the pies were served you always pointed out the pie you had made. After that everyone at your table chose your pie and congratulated you on the flaky crust and asked for the recipe. Reputations of the cooks were made or lost on the pies at the bean suppers.

All of the kitchen workers had a special job to do. There was the bean dipper who ladled out the hot beans into serving dishes. There was the bean dipper's helper who would clean off the edges of the bean dishes where the dipper over filled the dish. There was the coffee maker. There was a jellied salad server who had to be fast on her feet to get that Jell-O served before the Jell-O collapsed and became sauce. Whoever arrived last to help got the job of washing dishes. That's where you got wrinkled fingers and grease up to your armpits from the potato salad and the hot dogs. Actually, I liked being dishwasher because you got to make very important decisions such as whether to wash the plates first or the cups first and how often to change the dishwater.

We all had a good time at those bean suppers and they did make money. We socialized all winter with our friends over those baked beans.

Cranberry – Raspberry Salad...

24-30 Servings

Combine...
6 cups of boiling water
3 - 6 oz. boxes of raspberry jello

Chill until very thick but not set.

Beat in...
4 cups sour cream
2 – 1 lbs whole cranberry sauce

Divide into 2 molds or 2 - 13" by 9" pans

Chill until firm.

Good for a church supper.

Baked Beans...

To feed 135 to 150 people

20 pounds pea beans
20 pounds kidney beans

Use 2 medium pots and 2 large pots
Large pot is 14" in diameter and 12" high
Medium pot is 9" in diameter and 11" high

Fill pots **1/3** full of beans
¾ cold water
Soak over night.

Next day at 8 AM, keep the water that is left in the pots and fill with cold water until the beans are covered.

Add to large pot...
2 cups molasses
2 pounds brown sugar
4 tablespoons salt
4 tablespoons pepper
Divide 3 lbs. salt pork into 4 chunks.
Add one chunk to each pot.

Add to medium pot...
1 1/2 cups molasses
1 1/2 pounds brown sugar
2 tablespoons salt
2 tablespoons pepper

Betty Kennedy Tufts

Divide 3 lbs. salt pork into 4 chunks.
Add one chunk to each pot.

Cook in oven at 325 degrees until 2 PM, then turn down to 250 degrees for remaining time until about 4-4:30.

Recipe – Arthur Tufts

One Lump or Two…

Ever hear of the Silver Tea? Maybe not, but for many years, it was a genteel way for church ladies to raise money, and not only that, it was an elite social happening. In our church it took place in the vestry. For a week, these dedicated ladies baked and spread and frosted little cakes with buttery icing and topped off with a few of those round silver drages (that's what they were called in <u>Ladies Home Journal</u>). They sent an electric shock up your jaw if one of them hit a filling in your back teeth. Awful! The ladies also made dainty tea sandwiches with the crusts lopped off and a dab of some exotic filling. Everything was top drawer. Class.

The tables were covered with white linen tablecloths that had been boiled, bleached, starched and ironed. The long serving table was one of those pathetic home made jobs with legs of saw horses and tops of pine boards, everything put together with hinges that locked. You hoped and prayed during any event that the whole thing would not collapse. (Don't even think about it.) On the head table, the centerpiece was someone's houseplant, usually a begonia that had been forced to bloom for this occasion. They would spread a white doily around the pot to make it presentable. On either side of the plant were silver candlesticks, and on the end of the table was the cracker jack of it all, the silver tea service. Now it happened that two of the ladies of the group each owned one, so they took turns using one or the other. It was a tremendous honor for the tea service owner because she got to pour and we all know the great responsibility that is! She was next to God. That meant that she filled the bone china cups (these were borrowed, too) with tea and asked with silver sugar tongs poised politely in the air "… one lump or two?" of sugar. If you were really toney, you would ask for a slice of lemon.

All of these ladies wore their best garb, like sopranos in an operetta. They wore flowery silk dresses with white gloves, and of course and most importantly, big fancy hats. Sometimes there was one with life size red cherries bobbing in the air with every bite of cream cheese and olive sandwich that the wearer took. She would get first prize for <u>Hat of the Month</u> anywhere. Ladies in those days got a lot of mileage out of a fancy hat.

That was a Silver Tea, ladies donating silver coins for the pleasure of nibbling all the goodies that they had made themselves. The coins were then given to a current "good deed" project.

Betty Kennedy Tufts

Strawberries...

Put 2 small pkgs. or 1 large package of strawberry jello into bowl

Add...
¾ cup condensed milk to dry strawberry Jell-O. Mix well
Add...
1 teaspoon vanilla
1 cup coconut chopped fine
1 cup chopped walnuts

Mix well and refrigerate for an hour.

Form strawberries into the shape of real strawberries
Roll each strawberry in sugar
With a pastry tube decorate ends of strawberries with butter icing colored green and shape like leaves.

Refrigerate until serving.

These freeze well. They look lovely in paper soufflé cups and served with other sweets at a party.

Pink Ladies (Bars)...

Mix...
2 eggs well beaten
¾ cup sugar
1 ½ cups dates chopped
1 cup walnuts chopped
12 maraschino cherries cut up
½ cup flour
1 teaspoon baking powder
½ teaspoon salt
I small bag of little marshmallows

Put in 9" x 12" pan.
Bake at 350 degrees for 25 minutes.

Cut marshmallows in half and place upside down on top of the warm cake, as soon as it comes out of the oven. When cool, frost with butter icing flavored with almond and colored pink from cherry juice.
Makes 40 squares.

A very elegant bar for a ladies' luncheon
From Canada, 1945

Kid Stuff...

North Berwick was truly one of the best places for kids growing up. It was a nurturing, pleasant and fun place. Everyone knew everyone else, knew where everyone lived and knew where everyone had been.

In winter, kids young and old went skating down on the Frize on Elm Street. Going skating after school and every weekend, every one did. We girls sat on the granite wall beside the ice to put on our skates; but if you were lucky some boy who had a crush on you would help you lace them up. After that he might ask you to skate with him. The older boys would start a chain of skaters and play "Snap the Whip." If you could skate well enough, you joined the tail and hoped you could keep up with the others. It was fun to be on the end because you got whipped around like crazy and if you let go you'd end up under the bridge where the ice was thinner and the river deeper.

My skating ability was like all the sports I tried. Not very good. I was always the last one to be chosen for a sport. No one wanted to be stuck with me on their team. I was that bad. I thought those tubular skates I got for Christmas didn't help me much to skate like Hans Brinker. I don't know why skates were made like that. The tubes were heavy. I hope they don't make skates like that today.

The boys picked up old tires from all over town and burned them in great fires at the edge of the ice. It was wonderful to see the high flames dancing in the air and feel the warmth from the fire. No one paid any attention to the acrid smoke curling all over the neighborhood.

When the weather was really bad we had all kinds of things to do at home. We made fudge and corn balls and got burned on the hot taffy every time. We played Parcheesi and Jack Straws and jackstones on the kitchen linoleum. We mixed water and flour to make paste. We made scrapbooks; mine were of movie stars. I had Ann Harding, Mary Brian, Jean Harlow, Lew Ayres, Richard Barthelmas and of course, Rudy Vallee. We loved to hear Rudy say "Hi Ho everybody. This is Rudy Vallee." And then he went right into the *Maine Stein Song.* No one could sing that like Rudy and he was handsome, too, with wavy hair. We listened to Tom Mix and the cowboys on the radio and sent in box tops of Wheatena to get a Tom Mix ring. And then we all had to eat that gritty Wheatena which most of us hated.

In the spring, my crowd went on bicycle trips all over Bauneg Beg, Beech Ridge, Rooster Hill, Tatnic, Cabbage Hill, Beaver Dam and Rabbitborough. We tied our lunches on the handlebars of our bikes and sometimes included a fry pan. When we found a small gravel pit, we built a little fire to cook our hot dogs. (Can you imagine it?) I always brought along a cream horn - it was lots of lardy cream crammed into a lardy pastry roll. Sometimes we biked up to the Governor Goodwin place beyond Turkey Street. The house was in shambles then. I wonder if it is still there? Probably not. It has been over 65 years since we were there.

In the summer, we biked up to the pond – Bauneg Beg, that is, to a little sandy beach on the southern end owned by the Morrill family. Swimmers changed their clothes in the bushes and tied their wet bathing suits to the door handles on their cars, not giving a thought to how tacky and low rent it looked.

We had the Campfire Girls to join. There was a strong Boy Scout program, too. I don't know much about them. I only know that I was invited to 'Best Girl Night" once and it was nice. Sorry to say, I can't remember whose best girl I was.

Anyway, back to the Campfire Girls. Our group was formed by Viola Lowe who did so much for us over and over again. Each one of us girls chose an Indian name. Mine was Minneheca, which means <u>industrious</u>. I probably took the name to impress Miss Lowe or my mother, but I can't recall it ever made any change in me. We did all kinds of things to earn our colored wooden beads for our tribal necklaces. The red ones were for health and the red, white and blue ones were for citizenship and there were others.

We were so proud when our Campfire Girls group marched in the Memorial Day parade, behind the American Legion and the Boy Scouts. The route was from the middle of the town up High Street and Turkey Street to the "old" cemetery. That cemetery was beautiful and had been there for many years; enough years for the maple trees and pines to have heavy foliage. And that was the cause of the hold up in the parade in 1935. After prayers were said and taps were echoes and the marching was resumed, the Campfire Girls got their flag caught up in the branches of the maples. The whole parade shut down until a veteran marching with the American Legion up ahead came back down the line and freed the flag and us. It was not a good start on our citizenship bead.

One year, we put on a show in the Kezars' barn which had to be cleaned up first from Barbara's pet hens, Yaw Yaw and Queenie. Before the show, we wrote advertising leaflets, and Pauline McCrellis and I put them all over town; the drug store, the A & P and the barber shop. That was wishful thinking on our part. What customer having a shave and a haircut in Arthur Hooke's barber shop would ever be interested in reading a leaflet advertising a dumb production by kids put on in a barn with a bunch of admiring mothers? I guess that because I always went to Arthur Hooke's to have my hair shingled, I figured he might be interested. Back to the show. We had a full house, standing room only. Our loyal families and the minister came. I wish I could remember what the production was all about. It may have been a singing cowboy show. Gene Autry was beginning to be big then. We had the real goods; all of us.

We used the cash profit from the show for a trip to Dover on the train. There were six or seven of us twelve or thirteen year olds ready to take on a new adventure. We went to the movies to see

Ruby Keeler dance and hear Al Jolson sing and maybe a short subject of Laurel & Hardy. Our next stop was to Daeris' Tea Room where we ordered butterscotch sauce on vanilla ice cream served in shiny metal dishes. The trick was to eat the hot butterscotch sauce before it got cold and turned into a blob and sticky enough to loosen the fillings from your back teeth. We could handle that. We were up to it. We gave that butterscotch sauce a good challenge.

For me, and for most of the kids in North Berwick, we had a marvelous time being kids and doing kid stuff. We were lucky.

Betty Kennedy Tufts

Divinity Fudge...

2 2/3 cups sugar
1/3 cup white Karo Syrup
1/3 cup cold water
2 egg whites
1 cup nutmeats
1 teaspoon Vanilla or almond extract

Boil the sugar, syrup and cold water until a little of the mixture dropped in cold water forms a brittle thread. Beat egg whites stiff in a large bowl. Pour the hot syrup mixture over the egg whites slowly, beating constantly with an eggbeater. Add flavoring and nutmeats. Beat with a spoon until when poured in a pan it must be spread around.

Pearl Lincoln
1935

Corn Balls...

1 cup sugar
1 cup molasses
Scant 2 Teaspoons vinegar
Little salt

Mix together
Boil until brittle

Add...
1 teaspoon vanilla
A piece of butter
Pinch of soda

Pour over unsalted popcorn
Butter you hands before forming the mixture into balls

Mae Billings
1945
Kids love to make these.

Long Johns and Beach Pajamas...

Clothes were such a struggle for kids a couple of generations ago. No slacks, no tights, no ski parkas with hoods, nothing comfortable or sensible for cold Maine winters.

I always hated, come November, when we kids had to put on long stockings for the winter. Worst of all, you lost face if you were the first one in your class whose mother insisted on it at the first frost. The problem was we had to drag those ugly ribbed stockings over the bunchy stretched out long-legged underwear. Those were so lumpy that it was no secret to the world that you were wearing all that ungodly underpinning. First you put on the long johns. Then came the "waist," which was like a bullet proof vest only it was cotton and good for nothing except to hold up the stockings. There were long elastic garters fastened to the waist and then to the stockings. The plan then was to fold over the long legged underwear neatly (neatly was the key word here) so that the stockings could be pulled up over them. This was an every day challenge. Usually the stockings got baggy over the knees anyway. Eventually one or two garters got so stretched out that they let go and one stocking was left flapping and you hated it. You had to keep yanking and shifting the tops of the stockings to keep it decent. Boys in the grade school wore the same long stockings that we did, only with knee britches. I never did know what held their stockings up. Underwear never seemed to come up in our conversation.

Then came spring and the big day when you shed those miserable stockings. Now out came the girls' cotton dresses with those horrible matching bloomers with pockets like a kangaroo for your hanky. The whole drill was to have some of the bloomers in plain sight to set off the entire shooting match. Whose inspiration that was, I'll never know. Hankies played an important part in every ensemble. You never set foot out the door without your mother saying, "Do you have a clean handkerchief?" And you always said yes, whether you did or not.

Along with new spring dresses came the silk hair bow. At nine inches across, it was fastened to a thick hank of hair on the side. It really looked pretty snappy until you played jump rope; and then the bow got tangled into a big knot with rope and hair and you were in for a tough time straightening it out.

During this time, beach pajamas came out. They weren't pajamas for bed and they were too hot for the beach, but they really looked good. They were made of bright or colorful fabric and made with flared legs. This is probably the beginning of ladies' slacks. These were trendsetters.

When you scoff at the low waisted blue jeans or sloppy sweatshirts today, just think of my generation and know we wrestled with long johns and cotton stockings. Calvin Klein was never considered in our wardrobes.

Chocolate Cake...

1 cup sugar
1 cup sour milk
1 teaspoon soda dissolved in 3 tablespoons of hot water
½ cup cocoa

Mix together and add....
1 ½ cups flour
1-teaspoon vanilla
5 tablespoons melted butter

Mix all together
Bake at 350 degrees in 8" X 8" pan until it curls around the edges

This is a very moist rich cake.

Laura H. Tufts
1945
This was a great favorite of her grandchildren.

Betty Kennedy Tufts

Molded Tomato Aspic...

Something really different!

1 package lemon jello
¼ cups hot water
8 oz. can tomato sauce
½ tablespoon vinegar
½ teaspoon salt

Dissolve jello in hot water

Blend in remaining ingredients
Place in greased mold.

When partially chilled add…..
1 ½ cups chopped onion and celery
1 cup tiny canned shrimp.

Continue to chill.

How I Gave Up Smoking at Age 9...

I was a little kid in the 30s. My dad and I walked over town every Saturday night. Dad bought me a chocolate ice cream cone from Hurd's Drug Store, and for himself, a *Saturday Evening Post* and a Blackstone cigar. Since then I have always liked the smell of a burning cigar because it reminds me of Dad. And sometimes it reminds me of another cigar in my past.

One day when I bounced in from school, I found a very warm half-smoked cigar in a tin ashtray. Well, here was my lucky chance to try out one of Dad's cigars; to find out if it would be as good to smoke it, as it was to smell it. With the cigar in my hand like an old pro, I took a few drags on it and began to cough. Then I heard footsteps coming down the stairs. It was <u>Doctor Lightle</u> and it was HIS cigar that I had been rolling around in my mouth. I almost lost the Eskimo

Pie I just ate! I hastily jammed that cigar into the ashtray and prayed that he wouldn't notice it was hot. The doctor, a feisty old M.D. had been making a house call to my mother who was sick upstairs and I didn't know it. I was horrified when he picked up <u>his</u> cigar and went puffing on his way. Trying out my father's cigar was one thing, but puffing on Doctor Lightle's cigar was something else. I didn't even like Doctor Lightle. Mr. Personality, he was not. It cured me of ever smoking again and I have been content with the aroma of a good cigar instead of a trial run ever since. At age nine, I stopped smoking forever.

Twenty Minute Pound Cake…

2 cups sifted flour
½ cup shortening (butter is better)
1 ½ cup sugar
¼ teaspoon salt
2 teaspoons baking powder
4 eggs
1 teaspoon vanilla

Put everything n large bowl and beat 20 minutes
Pour into ungreased tube pan and place in cold oven.
Turn on oven to 350.
Bake for 1 hour.

Helen Hussey.

A Passenger for Mr. Sundstrom…

Mister Olaf Sundstrom, a farmer in town, had come from Sweden when he was young. He and his wife settled into a big farmhouse in town. They were quiet folks. They raised three children there and became part of the town. After every snowstorm it was Mr. Sundstrom's job to plow the sidewalks in the village. His rig was a big clumsy wooden plow painted in a heavenly shade of blue. It was pulled by a huge, tired, old white Belgian horse equipped with a leather harness and brass fittings. Mr. Sundstrom and his horse seemed to be well matched, the horse in his heavy winter coat and Mr. Sundstrom in his. I loved to watch that big old wonderful horse slog the plow through that heavy snow, leaving a perfect path behind.

Finally, one day I found the courage to ask Mr. Sundstrom for a ride. He grinned so wide I could count his back teeth. He helped me jump on board for a ride with him all over town, up Wells Street and down Portland Street, over to Elm Street and up High Street. There we were, Mr. Sundstrom holding the reins and clicking to the horse, while I held on to the front board. It was as good as a trip on the "Good Ship Lolly-Pop." I loved going through the town when we saw friends of mine look longingly for a ride when there was no more room on the plow.

There was one big mystery that puzzled me; Mr. Sundstrom would laugh with me and click to his horse, but he never talked. I knew he liked having me as a passenger, but why didn't he say anything? I talked to him in a running conversation. Then I told my father about it and it was plain to him: Mr. Sundstrom didn't speak English, only his native Swedish. That solved it and I finally understood my friend. I had many more rides with him and his proud old Belgian horse.

In the years that followed, Mr. Sundstrom's youngest son, called "Sonny," an Air Force pilot, was lost in World War II defending his father's adopted American country

Swedish Tea Ring…

Combine…
½ cup melted shortening
½ cup sugar
2 teaspoons salt
2 beaten eggs

Add…
1 pkg. Yeast dissolved in
½ cup lukewarm water

Add alternately…
2 cups scalded milk
7 cups flour

Knead lightly. Press into greased bowl. Cover with a damp cloth.
Let rise until double. Punch down. Divide into 2 parts. Let rest
for 10 minutes.

Form into two pieces. Roll each on floured surface to 12" by 24" rectangle. Brush with melted butter. Sprinkle with mixture of 1 cup sugar and 2 teaspoons of cinnamon.

Roll up each piece starting with the 24" side. Bring both ends together to form a ring and press ends together. Place on greased cookie sheet. With a sharp knife, cut at intervals of 2" and let rise again.

Bake for 25-30 minutes in 350 degree oven. This makes one large or two small rings.
Wait 5 minutes, then remove from pan. Decorate tea ring with icing, nuts and cherries.

Delicious and beautiful to look at.
1946

Swedish Meatballs...

Mix...
1 cup fine dry bread crumbs
1 lb. ground beef
½ cup ground pork
6 tablespoons finely chopped onion cooked until brown
½ cup milk
Add...
½ teaspoon pepper
½ teaspoon brown sugar
1 teaspoon salt
¼ teaspoon poultry seasoning
¼ teaspoon nutmeg
½ teaspoon allspice
Make into meatballs.
Cook in covered skillet with 3 table-spoons butter

Gravy
Remove meatballs from skillet, leaving liquid
Heat mixture until bubbly and blend 2 tablespoons of flour.
Add 1 cup cream
Return meatballs to pan
Simmer 30 minutes the gravy in the pan

Serve meat in gravy.

Merry-go-round…

Every summer we looked forward to our yearly trip to Old Orchard Beach with all its amusements: the rides, the food, the Pier and the frozen custard.

First – for me – it was a battle over what to wear on this exciting trip. My mother had a different idea than I. She insisted I wear a flowery organdy dress with ruffles. Now tell me how I could go slamming down that Jack and Jill slide on a burlap sack with that organdy dress on? But, like always, my mother won and I must say it didn't slow me down too much.

If you went by train, you got off in the middle of the main drag. And that's when you got all the aromas to sort out; the popcorn, the taffy in all those lovely pastel colors, the fried peppers and the hamburgers and the cotton candy. It was hard to pass them by, but we always headed for the frozen custard on the Pier. It was like soft ice cream but thick and creamy. I wonder what ever happened to frozen custard? We went screaming through the Old Mill where we had to walk through a revolving barrel and through the moving boardwalks. We took a ride in a little cart pulled by a sad little donkey down a scary "coal mine." We laughed and squealed when bursts of air blew our skirts over our knees. (I knew I didn't want to wear that dress.)

The merry-go-round was always fun but pretty tame after the Ferris wheel. And through it all, there was music everywhere, the band on the merry-go-round, the steel guitars on the Pier and the organ music at the Ferris wheel.

Many years later, I went to Old Orchard with my Navy JG husband. It was the summer of 1944. His ship was at the Navy base in Portland and we had some time together. We took a day, he and I, to go to Old Orchard and forget about the war and his return to the convoy making up for North Africa.

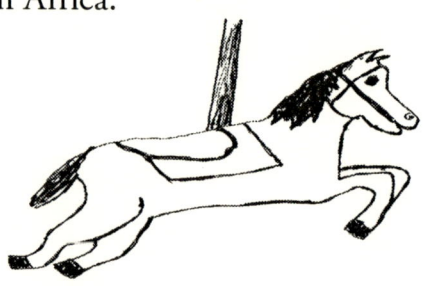

In spite of the wars all over the world, we found Old Orchard Beach hadn't changed, and we were glad that something had remained the same; the Pier, the "laughing woman" on top of the Old Mill, and the frozen custard. It was fun remembering when we were kids with no problems except that organdy dress.

Betty Kennedy Tufts

Frozen Custard...

2 cups milk
3 eggs beaten
¾ cup sugar
1/8-teaspoon salt
1 cup cream (whipped)
1 tablespoon vanilla

Heat milk in the top of the double boiler over boiling water
Mix...
Eggs
Sugar
Salt

Add the mixture to the milk stirring constantly until mixture thickens
Remove from heat and cool
When cooled, fold in whipped cream and vanilla
Pour into ice cube trays and freeze until firm.

Serves 6

Beneath the Sea Salad...

Dissolve
1 pkg. Lime Jell-O into
1 1/8 cups of hot water

Add...
½ cup pear juice
¼ teaspoon salt
1 teaspoon vinegar

Divide mixture in half

To one half of the Jell-O mixture add....
2 cups diced pears
Put into mold and chill until firm

To other half of mixture add...
2 large pkg. cream cheese softened
¼ teaspoon ginger

Beat well and pour on top of the other mixture in the mold.

Good and Pretty
Lancaster, New Hampshire
1960

The Village Smithy...

"Under the spreading chestnut tree the village smithy stands," said the poet. Well, we didn't have the chestnut tree, but we had the village blacksmith shop right beside our school grounds. It was Cliff Grant's shop where he worked, putting new iron shoes on all the horses in town. There were Belgians, riding horses, working horses and nags. The shop inside was dark and spooky and wildly fascinating where one or two horses stood patiently awaiting attention. Mr. Grant, with muscles like Arnold's, was a rugged middle-aged man with sweat – not perspiration; this was heavy-duty sweat running down his bald head. He let us come inside to poke around and watch. I won't say he actually invited us in, but the place was too good for an 11 year old to miss. How exciting it was to see him use the big bellows to pump up the flames in the open pit to heat the coals to their greatest peak. Then he would hold the shoe with the tongs over the flame until the iron shoe got fiery red. Only then could it be pounded into shape for that horse. When he figured it was just right, he plunged it into a vat of cold water. How that steamed and sizzled! It was something to see.

With the horse's hoof held on his heavy leather apron, Mr. Grant filed the hoof with a heavy rasp until it would fit the new shoe. While he was fitting the shoe, we kids would lean over, watching the action, completely mesmerized. He pounded in the heavy nails that held on the shoe. That hoof was done.

It was a great place for the nosey kids who went there. It was one of those adventures a kid never forgets, and with one of those long horseshoe nails that Mr. Grant gave us, we were winners – big time!

Betty Kennedy Tufts

Baked Rice Pudding…

1 quart milk
1 cup of rice
½ teaspoon salt

Combine and bring to a boil until rice is cooked
Add…
¾ cup sugar
2 eggs well beaten
2 cups Half and Half
Pour into a greased casserole dish.
Bake in 350-degree oven for an hour.

Hearty Pressure Cooker Stew...

Sauté in pressure cooker uncovered
1 to 2 lbs. of beef cubes

Add
2 – 12 oz. Cans of V-8 Juice
2 cups of water

Cut up and add
2 carrots
2 onions
2 stalks of celery
2 potatoes

Toss lightly together
Place pressure at 15 lbs.
After it jiggles, cook 10 minutes ONLY
Run cold water over top of pressure cooker to stop cooking

This is very savory and wonderful for a cold day.

1950

Sixteen Polliwogs...

Right next to our school (hard to miss; it was the only school in town.) and behind Cliff Grant's blacksmith shop was a very wet, mucky swamp teaming with hundreds of polliwogs that were ours for the taking. Using rusty old Del Monte peach cans, many of us collected those unlucky polliwogs, hoping to see them all turn into frogs. It said so in the science books that we had. It <u>never</u> happened. I had sixteen of them at my house, swimming around in my mother's washtub, without a thought in the world of being anything but a polliwog. Actually, I couldn't keep up with them because they died faster than I could get more. I also think they weren't doing much good to my mother's washtub because a slight layer of slime was building up on the sides.

My mother was glad they died before they turned into frogs. Now there is a horrible thought:

having sixteen full sized frogs jumping around loose in our shed amid the piled up magazines, the garbage cans, our winter boots, and overshoes, and the rag bag that hung on the wall. I can imagine how dear old dad would appreciate that.

Another thing, how many kids sat at their desks in school all day with muddy squishy shoes and wet socks down around their ankles. Many of us hid our cans full of swamp water and innocent polliwogs in our desks. We thought we were pretty safe in keeping our polliwog catching from our teacher until some careless kid jammed his geography book into his desk and dumped over the peach can and the flopping polliwogs into the leavings of his peanut butter sandwich left from his lunch. That was not a pretty sight. It really slowed us down for a few days. I'll tell you, we were some wild.

Betty Kennedy Tufts

Cape Cod Pot Roast...

4 lbs. Beef roll
4 tablespoons lard
1 small bottle of horseradish
Salt and pepper

Brown meat in hot fat.
Drain liquid from horseradish and   pour over the meat
Cook slowly about 2 or 3 hours
Add water from time to time

Leah Libby
1940

Corn Pudding…

1 can of corn
3 eggs lightly beaten
3 tablespoons melted butter
½ cup milk
Pinch of salt
2 tablespoons flour
Mix all ingredients

Pour into buttered baking dish

Bake in hot oven for ¾ of an hour.

Birtha Littlefield
1889

School's Out...

For the last day of school every year we had two ways to celebrate: a picnic in the Grove or a trip to Wells Beach. We took turns doing both from one year to another.

The Grove was a lovely pine needled glen in the woods behind Mary Hurd's estate. It was a grassy riverbank covered with moss around the edge. It was beside a small stream only about two feet deep of clean clear water that gurgled over the rocks. It was beautiful.

The whole idea of running and rambling down that wooded path and in the woods beside it with a noisy crowd of liberated kids was just the ticket for the last day of school. It also scared the daylights out of Bambi and Brer Rabbit. They beat it!

We swapped sandwiches: tuna fish for egg salad, ate olives, hard boiled eggs, and drank

Tales of North Berwick

homemade root beer bottled up in ketchup jars. Sometimes someone had a whoopie pie, which he did not share with anyone. It was his gem.

We tried to walk across the river on a pine tree log without falling in. This was a win-win affair. We won if we walked across the log without falling in (that made us very clever); we won if we fell in and got soaking wet. Everyone got a kick out of that. We looked good either way. Sometimes we found a Lady's Slipper or a Jack-in-the- Pulpit that we took home in our grubby hands. Maybe that's why they are on the "don't pick" list today.

The other last-day-of-school trip was to Wells Beach. A big part of the excitement was riding in the back of Ralph Littlefield's MACK truck – the one with the bulldog on the radiator cap. Wow! How good it was to have the air blowing in our faces and tangling our hair. No one said it wasn't safe.

We dashed madly into the ocean with the courage of Molly Brown when she left the Titanic. We almost died from shivering in that icy water, but we all bragged, with purple lips and full-blown shivers to the wimps how much fun it was.

We collected crabs and we played airplane and hopscotch on the beach. Once in a while a boy would draw a big heart on the beach and join his initials with those of his girlfriend with a big arrow drawn through them both. If the beach had a lot of seaweed, the boys flapped their friends with it. Wow! That was living in high cotton! I don't think suntan lotion was ever thought of then. Whenever we did get sunburned, we smeared calomine lotion all over our faces and bodies. It was white and we looked like clowns in the circus without the foot long shoes.

But one of the best parts of the last day of school was being allowed to wear <u>shorts</u>; and not only that; we could wear our bathing suits underneath. It was such a wonderful day for us.

Aggression Cookies...

Makes a lot for hungry kids

Mix
3 cups brown sugar
3 cups margarine or butter
6 cups oatmeal uncooked

Add...
3 cups flour
1 tablespoon baking soda

Place all of it into a big bowl.
Mash   Knead
Squeeze   Punch
Take out all of your aggressions

Form into small balls
Place on ungreased baking sheet
Mash down with bottom of a glass

Bake at 350-degree oven for 10-12 minutes

This makes a lot of cookies. Sometimes I frost with butter icing flavored with a little almond extract.
1960

Betty Kennedy Tufts

Pickled Eggs...

For a picnic

2 med. cans of tiny beets
10 hard cooked eggs
1-cup vinegar
Salt and pepper

Drain beets, saving juice.
Add
1 cup vinegar and about 1 teaspoon of salt

Place shelled eggs and beets in a bowl so that vinegar cover most of the eggs.
Cover and store in icebox for a day or two.

You will have pink pickled eggs.

Didn't you always want to know how to pickle eggs?
1940's

High School Came Next...

From the eighth grade we went on to high school. Not much of a change because it was the same building we'd been in for eight years. Didn't we know that now when we went to the basement (that's what we called the bathroom with five stalls), we didn't have to raise our hands to get permission; all we had to do now was "sign out" - but they were the same toilets.

Not only that, teachers didn't call us by our first names anymore, they called us Mr. or Miss and now we had to stand when we were giving an answer. We also had to stand when we didn't know the answer.

As we became upper classmen and had proved to be reliable, we claimed other important duties. Senior girls were asked to mind the principal's office when he was teaching a class. We answered the phone and rang all the bells for classes. How could we be more responsible than that?

Basketball was the big sport at NBHS in the 30's and 40's. In 1935 Leslie Marston came to teach math and coach basketball. He put new life into the teams. During that time sports had a great following of townspeople. On Tuesday or Friday nights the town all turned out for the game in Commercial Hall to see our teams in their new white satin uniforms, pretty flashy outfits. Those teams were to be reckoned with. They were <u>good.</u> We didn't have our own gym or bleachers or showers, just those ugly folding seats that collapsed with no warning on 3 or 4 loyal mothers who went to every game.

Other schools had their gym problems, too. Wells played in the hall over the store; Kennebunkport and Eliot both used halls (maybe Grange Halls) out in the country with a woodstove at one end and a wide open door at the other end. It was a great run for some aggressive players who were carried away by the crowds to keep going with the ball right out that door into a snow bank. That's the nearest thing they had to a shower.

Players all went to their games in private cars, with some parents and others. That was another adventure because girls and boys were mixed passengers. You just cannot imagine what fun that was.

After an away game we usually stopped at a diner for soda or a piece of pie. (These are Maine kids remember). We went to Jones Diner in Kennebunk and the Red Arrow in Wells. Being on the basketball teams, girls and boys had big advantages over and above being a good player. There were all those fringe benefits.

Betty Kennedy Tufts

Grapenut Pudding…

1 quart of scalded milk
1 cup grape nuts
3 eggs beaten
1 cup sugar
½ teaspoons salt
1 teaspoon vanilla

Scald milk
Remove from stove and add grape nuts. Allow to soak until cool.

Add…
Beaten eggs
Sugar
Salt
Vanilla

Bake 30 minutes
Serve with whipped cream

Cookbook
1935

Tingie Mows Down a Heifer...

Tingie (Roscoe) Littlefield was the only kid in high school who owned a car; a 1927 Chevy, and Tingie was generous with it. We all loved that old car that could have a life of its own. One day when there was a car full of us, Tingie drove down Central Avenue in Dover and one of the back doors came loose and fell off. It had been losing ground for quite a while. He also had a cowbell on the back and it clunked every time he drove over a bump in the road, which was all the time. Tingie really didn't need the cowbell to get attention. That old Chevy spoke for itself.

One day after senior play practice, Tingie offered a ride to Richard Day to his home in Bauneg Beg. Since the trip was quite long, we all jumped in for the ride. Happily tooling along the

Valley Road at a good clip, Tingie bowled over a cow that wandered into the road. That cow never had a chance with the Chevy. The cow was done for. I went with Tingie to the nearest farm, Day's place, where the cow belonged. Freemie Day was not all that happy to lose one of his herd of Holsteins. Can't say he was exactly kicking up his heels to forgive Tingie nor even to understand how the accident came about. All he saw was a carload of irresponsible kids, an old junky automobile and his dead cow. Not fun turning himself in, Tingie then called his father, Roy Littlefield, and said "Dad I just mowed down one of Freemie Day's heifers. What shall I do?" His father said, "Come home" in not a happy mood. Another adventure in the old Chevy.

The year was 1940.

Marion Littlefield's Baked Turnip…

This was Tingie's Mother

Take 2 cups cooled mashed turnip
Add…
2 eggs separated
1 small onion minced
Salt and pepper
Fold in 2 egg whites, which have been beaten well

Bake in a greased casserole dish about 20 minutes

Every one in town eventually cooked their turnip this way.

Marion Littlefield
1940

Remember Prize Speaking...

Prize Speaking was more than a presentation given by our high school students at the Congregational Church every spring. It was WORK. During the winter every student in high school – except the seniors – had to learn a "piece" to speak in English class. These were try-outs for prize speaking presentation in May. Now there are some people who go for this stuff and love melodrama in a big way. They can declaim so forcefully that half the audience is ready to sign up for the United States Marine Corps and serve. Then there are those who despise every line they have to learn and almost throw up before they can get up before an audience and say anything, not just the piece they had to learn. From the pool of these speakers, eight were chosen for the big contest. Each speaker could choose his own presentation and that created some variety in the program. In 1936 Elroy Littlefield spoke dramatically "The Tell-Tale Heart." I think that was about the crook whose heart beat so loudly that his guilt gave him away. Then one year Natalie Kennedy spoke "Ma at the PTA" and Buddy Magee had for us "The Highwayman." That was long before Willie Nelson taped it. I will never forget the "Tlot Tlot, and the Highwayman came riding."

One year, we came close to disaster when two of the contestants showed up for the contest wearing identical new dresses from the Sears Roebuck catalog. Those dresses were hard to miss. They were two piece navy blue affairs; a flowered dress with a long net jacket over it and sporting a whipped up artificial flower on the shoulder. One at a time, these dresses had a lot of charm, but two of them were a tad overdone. These two girls were to speak one after the other. Not to worry, Miss Guptill went to work and changed the order of the program. One was to be first and the other was to be last. You never know when a tragedy of great significance can be avoided by smart people.

Three out-of-town judges awarded the prizes after our school's six piece orchestra played a few painful numbers like "Swanee River" and "Camp town Races." What a night it was for these speakers and their audience. Who knew what drama could come after this?

Graham Cracker Pudding...

4 graham crackers soaked in 1 pint of milk
Add…
 2 egg yokes beaten
½ teaspoon cinnamon
½ teaspoon nutmeg
1 tablespoon butter

Bake for 45 minutes at 350 degrees

To serve:
Beat 2 egg whites
Add ½ cup powdered sugar

Spread over the top of pudding
Brown slightly in oven.

Georgina Day
1945

Tales Out of School...

Our school in North Berwick was a square two-story brick no- nonsense building. It was arranged for nine years of grade school and four years of high school, two grades in each room, all the way up. It really was an advantage to have two grades in one room. If you were in the lower year you could get a head start on next year; if you were in the upper grade you could coast all year because you had already heard it all. Actually, you could say we were exposed to the same subject twice.

The classrooms were Spartan. No decoration at all. They were plain cream color walls and dark wood floors that had been oiled for so many years they were black. Our janitor, Mr. Lowe, strewed the floor with green, oily compound that looked like sawdust. Then he swept everything up at once, including all the dried mud that had been dragged in by the kids who had been in the swamp catching polliwogs.

The only attempt to decorate these rooms at all were the sepia prints in big frames on the walls. There were "The Signing of the Declaration of Independence" and "Washington Crossing the Delaware". There also was Rosa Bonheur's painting," The Horse Fair". I looked at that painting for two solid years and those horses never made any headway as far as I could see.

There was no color in these rooms at all. That could make for a dull day if you didn't provide your own and some of us were pretty good at that. Our desks and chairs were screwed firmly to the floor. (There were two generations of chewing gum under the desks.) We were lucky these seats didn't have seat belts.

Classes were small and we came in for some close attention. All bases were covered. We couldn't chew gum (why was that such a deadly sin?) No eating. No note passing, no communicating (Miss Lowe's word) with your neighbor, no talking. In spite of all that, we did some pretty silly things, which we thought were hilarious at the time. In the 30s, when organized labor came into its own, a new way of holding a strike was to sit down on the job and refuse to move. It was called a sit-down strike and that's what we did in the eighth grade when we didn't like the teacher. We had a plan. That teacher jawed at us kids all the time; her lessons were as dull as orthopedic shoes. She was a clunker as far as we were concerned. So one day we all sat there with hands and heads down on the desks, not moving. We thought we were pretty slick – until the principal came in. We lost – <u>big time</u>. Another time Stan Thompson put salt fish in the heating blowers. The air in that room got pretty ripe but we acted like we couldn't smell a thing. Or the time someone threw my shoe out the window in algebra class. We thought Mr. Marston would blow his top and pace around the room telling us all we had a bad attitude. But he didn't. He just calmly told me to go get it. It spoiled all of the fun.

I liked most everything in school subjects except penmanship and singing in "Notes" in Music. In penmanship, I know it's a good thing to write well, but I could never figure out how making those ovals round and round and making those push pulls up and down taught me very much. Those classes were about as wild as grape Kool Aid. And would you believe it, we had to position our feet flat on the floor just so. Then the teacher would go around the room flattening our wrists to the desktop while we were writing. That was the Palmer Method and I don't believe Palmer ever was a kid. How could you hold your pen up straight if you kept your wrist flat down? You try it. How could all this matter when I was only trying to write my name? Doctors don't write very well and see how smart they are.

Our music teacher was Azalea Watson. I remembered her name because it was so beautiful, but can you imagine someone named Geranium? But you would remember it. We knew we were in for it when Miss Watson came into the room and drew lines on the blackboard with that funny little chalk holder that would draw 5 lines all at once. We were going to learn and sing in syllables. You know – like do-re-me and so on. I hated those. I never heard anyone in my life going around singing "Home On The Range" in syllables. I always heard words.

I was relieved when Miss Watson brought in the blue leatherette wind-up victrola. It was the kind that sounded funny when it was running down. Actually, she played some pretty weird records on it, too. I always hoped she'd play some plain old folk songs, the kind you could sing like "Danny Boy" or "A Capital Ship."

Still, I have to say very strongly that my education in that school showed up to be the best when I went to college with kids from big schools in Maine. We must have been doing something right in our schools in North Berwick and I loved that school.

Oven Barbecued Spare Ribs...

4 lbs. Spare ribs
2 onions sliced
Salt and Pepper

Place in roaster

Barbecue Sauce

Combine and heat...
2 onions sliced
1 can tomato soup
¾ cup water
3 tablespoon vinegar
2 tablespoons Worcestershire sauce
1-teaspoon salt
¼ teaspoon cinnamon
1 teaspoon paprika
¼ teaspoon black pepper 1/8-teaspoon cloves

Pour sauce over ribs.
Cover pan
Cook 1 ½ hours at 350 degrees
Remove cover and roast 20 minutes longer.

Serve over cooked rice.

The 1940 Jet Set...

A senior class trip to Washington in the spring was the greatest time of all. We looked forward to it during all our years in high school. We worked hard all winter raising money for our trip. We put on a play "A Pair of Country Kids" in which I was Hi and Maxine White was Sis. We put all we had into those roles; Maxine and I were positively country kids. We had a good time. We had food sales; we sold fudge, chocolate or peanut butter cookies, or anything else we could get our hands on. We also had whist parties when our parents took charge. We were only to show up to do the dishes. That meant that about six of us in Tingie's Chevy had two hours to kill. Not a problem! We had just enough time to drive down to the Nubble lighthouse at York Beach and wait for the red light to turn green. It never did. All those tourists who travel down to the Nubble these days just cannot know the secrets of that 1940 crowd.

The girls all got new outfits for the trip, in the color of the year as described by the *Boston Globe*. One year, 1939 it was thistle. The next year, 1939, was chartreuse, an ugly green. Our year 1940 was teal blue. We were all decked out like a freckle right down to the white pigskin gloves and straw hats we ditched before we got ten miles down the tracks to Dover. And the boys? They had new bunchy reversible topcoats and new soft hats. They ditched their hats in Dover, too.

We left North Berwick on the 12:20 train. That was really pretty nice because everybody in town came to the depot to see us off during their lunch hour. What a responsibility for us to look good when all these townspeople were risking being late to the Mill at one o'clock. Kids from some other nearby towns were already on the train and hanging out the windows to check us out. Many an out-of-town romance started that very day.

We climbed the Washington Monument, visited the U.S. Mint, had our pictures taken at the Capitol, and went to the Smithsonian. My favorites were the Lincoln Memorial and Mount Vernon. We tried to see it all.

That trip was where we earned our stripes as the Jet Set, although that name was unknown then. We rode in taxis for the first time, ate in fancy hotel dining rooms for the first time, and – Horrors! – sometimes had that first cigarette. My frivolity was changing my pageboy hairdo to look like Veronica Lake – hair down over one eye and over the shoulder. Very smart I thought, feeling like a movie star when I walked into that hotel dining room, until one of the boys asked me if I was trying to cover up a black eye. He was hopeless. What did he know about style anyway?

The trip was more than just a trip for our class. From the time when we took off those hats in Dover until we arrived back home a week later, we were the cat's meow. We had seen the world.

Scalloped Oysters...

1 ½ cups coarse cracker crumbs (Use Waverley crackers)
8 tablespoons melted butter
1 pint oysters
½ teaspoon salt
Pepper to taste
¼ cup cream
Dash of Tabasco sauce

Mix melted butter with crackers crumbs and spread in a thin layer in an 8" x 8" pan.

Add layer of oysters with juice & ¼ cup of cream

Sprinkle with remaining cracker crumbs

Bake for 30 minutes in 450-degree oven.

These are the <u>best</u>!

Betty Kennedy Tufts

Crab Cakes in Washington D.C....

Mix together…
2 eggs beaten
2 slices of white bread cut in ½" cubes

Add…
1 lbs. Crabmeat
1 tablespoon mayonnaise
1 teaspoon Dijon mustard
1 teaspoon horseradish
A little minced parsley

Form patties and fry in butter.

The Washington Post
1970

I Had the Itch...

One of the worst health problems ever to be dealt with in our family was curing me of scabies – THE ITCH. I had baby sat for a newly adopted 5-year-old boy who had arrived from out of state. Apparently this little boy had brought the itch right along with him and had passed it along to me. My family was horrified thinking of the talk around town if anyone got wind of it. I thought I would die of disgrace and my mother not far behind. I was 15 years old and just making my way with the social circle in high school. I would be another "Typhoid Mary." I had to scratch when no one was looking and that was hard because I itched all over, but especially my hands. It helped to smear my hands with a strong ointment and wear white gloves all the time. I told every body I had poison ivy but I looked like an end man in a minstrel show. All I lacked was a tambourine to go with those white gloves.

A doctor in Dover told my mother to wash every single article of my clothing and my bedding every single day. He told me to use Lysol on every inch and itch on my body. You can just imagine the wafts I gave off every time I moved. The worst time was when I was with a group of girls at school and Gloria Miniutti; the nicest and most popular upper classmate asked, "Can you smell disinfectant? Where is it coming from?" and I said,"I can't smell a thing." Imagine my dismay to have Gloria even suspect the smell was coming from me. I was just getting to know her and be counted as one of her friends. I felt just awful. I itched and itched and itched and I gritted my teeth not to scratch.

So off to Portland we went to a skin specialist. (This was calling in the big guns.) That specialist said we had been treating this condition all wrong; clean clothes every day was giving those microbes a fresh target every day to chew on. The new cure for me was to wear the same clothes-inside and out- every day for 2 weeks, or until the scabies got tired of the same old clothes and just quit and moved on.

Now I had a new problem; wearing the same clothes all the time; unheard of for a high school girl. The warm September days didn't help either – just more itching. Every day my mother would say, "Did anyone see you scratching?" "Did anyone ask you why you were wearing the same clothes?" Eventually the scabies did go away and my family's name for cleanliness intact. And I guess my friend never knew just what my problem was. My friendship with Gloria was safe and I was glad to take off those white gloves.

Betty Kennedy Tufts

Barbecued Hot Dogs...

2 lbs hot dogs cut diagonally into 1" pieces
¾ cup chopped onion
2 tablespoons vinegar
2 tablespoons brown sugar
¼ cup lemon juice
1cup ketchup
3 tablespoons Worcestershire sauce
¾ cup water

Combine all ingredients except hot dogs

Simmer 20 minutes

Add hot dogs and simmer slowly for 15-20 minutes stirring now and then.

Great for a party
1960

Poor Quasimodo...

I first met Quasimodo in French Class when we read "The Hunchback of Notre Dame." Quasimodo was the hunchback man who swung around the gargoyles of the cathedral in Paris and raced around the rafters looking after Esmeralda the gypsy girl he had fallen in love with. A noble undertaking. That drama may sound pretty interesting, but try reading the whole thing in French. It loses something. We did our best figuring out the plot and rescuing poor Quaismodo from a menacing crowd, but translating one word at a time was lost on us.

The most interesting part of that class for me was finding a note from my boyfriend inside my desk. He sat at the same desk in the calculus class during the period before. He always left a note for me, usually an invitation to stand around the coat racks in the corridor during recess, sharing a candy bar. Those notes and the candy bar really amounted to a lot. The note writer and I got married a few years after that and spent 46 years sharing candy bars.

I really wish I had studied that French a lot more, and therein lies a tale. About fifteen years after commiserating with Quasimodo and his lot in life in the cathedral, I found myself teaching French at Pembroke Academy in New Hampshire. Two teachers before me had given up the job as they thought it was too tough. Teaching all four classes of Track Two English, I could do, but for French Two, all I had was three years of high school work. The Head Master assured me I could do it when he asked me to take the job. Yes, I managed it by staying one lesson ahead of the class.

The English classes were also a challenge. Many of the students spoke French at home and English did not come easily to them. Grammar, for most boys was a drag and those sophomores at Pembroke Academy were not the exception. I remember one day I told my class we would be studying grammar the next week. The boy in the front row said to me very quietly, "This is where you loses me, Mrs. Tufts."

I was glad that my NBHS classes had been the best for me.

Margaret's Rigatoni…

Fry…
1 lb. cut up sausage
When half done add….
1 chopped onion

Add…
½ teaspoon nutmeg
¼ teaspoon oregano
¼ teaspoon poultry seasoning
Salt and pepper
1 can tomatoes
1 can tomato sauce

Simmer 1-2 hours.

Cook 2 handfuls of rigatoni and add to sauce,

1960

Gallia Est...

When I took Latin II it was tough because there were only three of us in the class. We three girls sat in the front row facing our teacher Marion Quarrington. We had to know each lesson; there was no one to hide behind when we hadn't learned all those Latin verbs.

For me, there was another problem. That class was just before lunch and I was always hungry, and my stomach talked. It rumbled and rumbled very loudly. We were in a nearly empty classroom – only four of us – and that rumble was like a sonic boom to me as it echoed around and around. I was so embarrassed. Whenever I could hear it start, I coughed, I cleared my throat, slammed my feet on the floor – whatever. The good part of it was the other two students and Mrs. Quarrington were so carried away with Gaul (France in the early days of the Roman Empire) and its problems that they didn't notice mine. But then one day, Mrs. Quarrington said I was not ladylike to be so noisy. I didn't know whether she meant the rumbling of my stomach or the slamming I was doing to cover it up.

About all I got out of that course was "Gallia est omnis divisa in partes tres". It says, "All Gaul is divided into three parts". Now right there is something you want to hang onto. Who knows when you'll be introduced to a new acquaintance in your neighborhood who speaks only Latin? You can always speak up and say in a very scholarly way "Gallia est omnis divisa in partes tres" and the whole crowd will be impressed and say how smart you are. I haven't met anyone like that yet, but I keep practicing "Gallia est…." Who knows when I'll meet the Pope?

Betty Kennedy Tufts

Chocolate Crinkle Cookies...

Makes about 50 cookies

Mix together...
½ cup cooking oil
4 squares unsweetened chocolate
2 cups sugar

Add...
2 eggs one at a time
Add...
2-teaspoon vanilla

Stir in...

½ teaspoon salt
2 cups flour
2-teaspoon baking powder

Chill for a time in the refrigerator
Roll into balls, and then roll in sugar

Place in greased baking sheet
Bake 10-12 minutes in 350-degree oven

Kids love these.

Big Doings in Commercial Hall...

Commercial Hall was a town fixture, serving well the generations of theatricals, town meetings, graduations and basketball games. It was the meeting place and gymnasium for the town. No one can forget that heavy painted canvas stage curtain showing off some sort of Tuscan scene (it sure wasn't from around here) of a woman in flowing robes, carrying a big jug of who knows what on her head. Right smack in the middle of that woman's get-up was a good-sized peephole. It got bigger every performance when one of the thespians spied on the audience. And was it a "standing room only" show?

We all got our diplomas from high school in that hall. Graduates, on the first night of our graduation filed onto the stage to the solemn beat of Hazel Guptill's rendition of Elgar's *Processional.* Not a dry eye in the place thinking of these young people facing the cruel world out there. For us it was a real parting. Most of us had been together from the first grade until graduation. We knew each other's middle names, each other's birthdays, our scars and what food we liked. We had been like family and now it was over. Then came the war years of the 40s when it was really sad to think of these young men leaving town on Monday to join up.

At graduation time, the seniors spent a week decorating that old landmark with yards and yards of rolled crepe paper in our class colors. Someone had built a fence along the front of the stage and covered it with evergreen branches. Then the letters of our class motto made of colored cardboard were woven into the greenery. If the motto didn't have many words in it, it looked pretty good. Ours, in 1940, was "Only a Beginning." We thought that was inspiring and it was pretty easy to read in all the shrubbery. It was a lot of fun decorating the hall when we did it on our own, without directions from the staff. Later on, when Al Sim came to town and started a carnation business, we got hundreds of his flowers to decorate the hall. They were fresh and sweet smelling and definitely a cut above the crepe paper that had been stretched out so much that sometimes it silently let go onto the crowd in the middle of our class song or during the Invocation.

The second night was the reception, which was the closest thing to a prom. All the seniors stood in a receiving line in front of the stage. We girls dressed beautifully in formal gowns and carried bouquets. The boys got to have a flower in the buttonholes of their jackets. The line of congratulations was followed with a grand march for which we had been coached. Then it was a proud time when fathers danced with their daughters. I was lucky because my Dad always liked to dance, and here was his opportunity to show me just how a waltz should be done. I loved it and I think he did too.

Richard Hurd ran silent movies in Commercial Hall until talkies came in 1928 or 1929. Everyone who could put together the price of a ticket took in the show on Saturday night. Along with the silent screen show, someone was paid to play piano music all through the production. When an exciting dilemma came on the screen; maybe the heroine tied to the railroad tracks by the villain, or when the big saw came nearer and nearer to Vera, the tempo quickened and the piano player gave all she had to play loud crashing music. Then when the love scene was on, the music was sweet and tender. Dick Hurd's piano player was Mrs.

Dockam, a lady of uncertain age and marcelled hair. She was fair game to the audience in the darkened hall, dodging pieces of candy or grapes or whatever. At the time those flying objects hit their mark, a livid Mrs. Dockam stopped her playing with a dischord and jumped up from her piano seat and bellowed in an unladylike yell, "Mr. Hurd, Mr. Hurd, make them stop firing stuff!"

The lights would go on and Mr. Hurd, like a bantam rooster, would hop onto the stage and bawl out the crowd and threaten to stop the show if the crowd didn't settle down. There was interesting action at that show, both on and off the screen.

For many years, the annual town meeting was held in Commercial Hall where all the legal voters met and had their say on any issue to come before the meeting. People whom you hadn't seen for a year came out of the woodwork to vote. The meeting was under the leadership of the Moderator, always elected first when the meeting started. They discussed their roads, their sidewalks; aid to the poor and of course, the school and where ever money was raised to defray town expenses. It was a moment to remember when someone stood up and had his say about the rotten job of plowing snow on his road. The town road commissioner came up for pot shots about any potholes in the highway. People who had no knowledge at all of the heavy equipment cast their vote pro or con. It was a time when anyone could shine and be important in our true democracy.

Phil Hussey always could be counted on to give a speech about our schools. He asked and pleaded every year for a new school with its own gymnasium. We appreciated what he had to say. Finally, in 1949 the new high school on High Street was opened. I remember it well because I was the new eighth grade teacher that year and was proud to have my class the first one in that new school. I had 10 boys and 10 girls – such great kids – the best I ever had!

I was lucky to have my classroom at the end of the corridor, but Hazel Guptill, the English teacher, was not so fortunate. Her room was actually the stage for the auditorium, having one wall of wood partitions that could slide open for the gym or closed for the class held on the stage. When the gym class was playing basketball, that ball got slammed wham on that wooden partition and shook up whatever class was on the other side. There was no doubt that some of that barrage was intentional to give that English class a little excitement during a dull lesson on infinitives and participles. You can't make custard without breaking the eggs. (Actually, that saying has absolutely nothing to do with this tale, but I think it's just great and I've wanted to use it for a long time.)

This new high school marked the beginning of growth in North Berwick schools.

Blueberry Pancakes...

In a large bowl combine...
1 cup flour
¼ teaspoon salt
½ teaspoon mace
1 tablespoon sugar
1 tablespoon baking powder

Mix together and add...
1 egg
1 cup milk
2 rounded tablespoons of sour cream

Add 2 tablespoons melted butter
Fold in 1 cup of blueberries.

This is the very best recipe for pancakes.

The Brits...

Most of the folks in North Berwick were native state-a-Mainers. So it was interesting to us when in the 1930s, Kirk Verity, a middle aged Englishman, became the designer for North Berwick Woolen Company. He and his wife Miriam were from England and despite the years they spent in the USA they remained British in many ways.

Mr. Verity, with his distinctive small, waxed moustache and his courtly manners, and Mrs. Verity, the proper English lady, were highly respected and admired by their friends and neighbors. We lived next door. Mr. Verity kept the sidewalks in front of their house and ours swept and neat. Wearing his dark suit coat and matching trousers, he never wore sport clothes or short sleeve shirts or jeans and sneakers. Perish the thought! His only departure from correct decorum was not wearing a necktie when he swept the cement.

Tales of North Berwick

One summer after Mrs. Verity had broken her ankle, I spent mornings with her helping with the cooking of her British dishes. I was never crazy over her hot cucumbers in white sauce, but I did love her Yorkshire Pudding, which I made for my family long afterward.

I spent a lot of time with Mrs. Verity when I was growing up. She and I had wonderful conversations about school and church and my friends. She was a great supporter of all my doings. When I got married, she and Mr. Verity rode the train to Boston just to buy her hat for the wedding. In the Boutique at Filenes', she bought a large navy blue hat with a wide brim all around, covered with silk lilies of the valley. It was a gorgeous creation, I was so proud of them at the wedding; my gracious British lady and her husband, Mr. Verity, my elegant friend. The highest praise from Mr. Verity was "champion!" and he and his Miriam were champion people.

ND*Yorkshire Pudding...

Beat well 2 or 3 eggs (eggs must be fresh)
Add…
1 cup milk
1 cup flour
½ teaspoon salt

While preparing the egg mixture, place a longish buttered cake pan to heat in the hot oven…450 degrees

Now turn the egg mixture into the pan with hot butter.
Bake at 400 degrees until the mixture puffs high on the sides and is slightly brown

Serve immediately with beef gravy.

Mrs. Miriam Verity
1941

North Berwick Puts on the Dog...

As far as style was concerned, North Berwick was right up there. Whatever was showing in the newsreels at the movies, or in the Boston papers, or in the catalogs, was in and that was for us. Maybe you heard about these.

1. <u>Alice Allen's Cape.</u> Mrs. Allen was a tall lady, and always at the top of fashion. When she wore her black and white hounds tooth wool cape she looked marvelous.

2. <u>Gone with the Wind Dresses.</u> When we were reading the book "Gone With The Wind" in 1937 before the movie came out, Ruth Swett and I bought those hot-looking dresses. Ruth's dress was blue and red and white and mine was aqua and brown and white...the same model. Each one had a flared skirt, coming from 10 or 12 gores around the waist. With those dresses and our saddle shoes, we thought we were fashion

plates. We looked good enough to be on Grand Old Oprey.

3. <u>Fascinaters</u> You couldn't know what these were unless your aunt had made you one. They were large triangular crocheted wool scarves. The idea was that when you were wearing one, you were fascinating to look at, even if you had a face like a bloodhound. What made them interesting was the very open crocheted pattern. It didn't keep your head too warm, and it wasn't much good in a snowstorm because the snow sifted down through the pattern, leaving a fancy design of snow on your head. In spite of that, everyone had to have one, but they went out of style like those pink flamingos on lawns.

4. <u>Bush Jackets</u> (Nothing to do with you know who.) These were white duck jackets, fingertip length and belted smartly at the waist. With big pockets in them, they looked like those worn on safaris in Africa in the bush country. What made these so wonderful was the autographs written all over them by your friends. With the sleeves rolled up a bit and the waist cinched in by the belt, they were killers.

5. <u>Snowsuits.</u> I think the one my mother made for me was a red style setter. It was one piece with a long zipper down the front. It was made of heavy woolen fabric from the mill. Actually that cloth was as stiff as a board but it kept out the snow and was very warm. When you climbed into it

Tales of North Berwick

you were ready for anything, except moving very fast.

6. Cloches. These were the hats of the 20s and 30s. The name came from the French and maybe the hats did, too. They were ultra chic. Every movie star who had her picture taken on board an ocean liner headed for Europe was wearing one and had several other colors in her steamer trunk. Cloches fit snug and didn't leave as much as a spit curl showing. I think the last time I saw someone wearing one was at the first Nixon inauguration.

7. Pongee Dresses. Made of an ecru color rough silk, these were Sunday school dresses. They looked really good too if you wore some other color with them.

8. Ski Pants and Ski Boots. Now everyone knows what they are, but did you know girls wore them to school and sat in those itchy woolen pants and heavy clomping boots all day? The boots were very plain lace up type with a hard box toe, not the elaborately engineered ones worn today. Usually the pants were held up by suspenders, which didn't add much to the look, either. They weren't for the weak and timid, you can be sure of that.

9. Dirndl Dresses. These numbers were patterned after those worn by Swiss girls in the Alps. They were gathered around the waist to a fitted top and if you were wore one three days in a row, you started to yodel, singing *Ricola* like the cough drops ad.

10. Snuggies.   These were girls' and womens' underwear. They were much nicer and prettier than the union suits we had been wearing when we were younger. The snuggies were made of pink stretchable cotton. They came in two pieces, tops and bottoms. Not too great in the fashion department, but warm. Unfortunately, these snuggies added one whole size to your clothes. It was like instant padding. I always think of these when I see pictures in the "National Geographic" of Chinese farmers. They always wear padded outfits, too; only their body suits are on the outside. Snuggies were always covered up and you never really knew the size of the girl until springtime when those snuggies were retired.

Calico Beans…

Sauté and brown in a large pan…
½ lb. bacon until crisp
Remove bacon. Save fat in pan
Sauté 6 sliced onion in fat and add to bacon

Mix together…
½ cup brown sugar
¼ cup vinegar
½ cup chili sauce
1-teaspoon mustard

Toss in with bacon and onions.

Add…
1 can Campbell's beans and tomato sauce
1 can lima beans
1 can butter beans
1 can kidney beans
Do not drain the beans

Stir all together and simmer. Do not let the beans get mushy.

This is from 1991…not so old but so good!

Sure Cures...

Every household had its own ideas about treating burns, bug bites, black eyes, upset stomach and "The Itch." Usually no one went to the hospital except for appendicitis or a cracked head. Every family treated its own. These were the common remedies. Read on –

1. Cloverine Salve came in a small round tin box painted white with green cloverleaves all over the top. It was bland. It may not have healed anything faster, but it smelled good. We figured we were doing something about that blister on the heel that we got from wearing new shoes on the first day of school after going barefoot all summer.

2. Beefsteak on a black eye. The chemical reaction here between the protein in the steak and the sore eye is lost on me. I never could figure that out. Anyhow, if everything else had been applied to the eye and didn't work, why not try the sirloin steak?

And it looked debonair, too. Women couldn't resist this kind of a guy.

3. Camphorated oil for a cold. Mothers saturated a little flannel bag with the stuff and hung it around your neck. You prayed that no one would see it; but that pungent smell followed everywhere you went. You sure didn't smell like Easter lilies. Rubbing your chest with camphorated oil was a last resort after you had been smeared with Vapo-Rub. This camphorated oil treatment either knocked the cold out of you or it turned into pneumonia and that was dreaded stuff. Then it was up to Doctor Lightle.

4. Witch Hazel? Which Hazel. Which Hazel do you mean? So goes the old jingle. Nice smelling witch hazel rubbed on sore muscles and patted on an aching head was soothing. Nobody ever expected a medical breakthrough in using it; but it was very calming and cool.

5. Mustard and hot water. If you had a really bad upset stomach or if you really needed to throw up, you got a vile mixture of dry mustard mixed with hot water. That was sure to do the trick. It lifted everything back three days. It went clear to your boot taps. It was wicked stuff.

6. Spirits of ammonia was always kept on hand for the weak and faint. One whiff of that brought you to your senses. In some cases a little ammonia on a spoon with sugar calmed your nerves. Probably the sugar set you up instead of the ammonia.

7. Grammie's rock. My grandmother kept a small rough white rock beside the soap at the sink. This was used to rub any stain off your hands. It was fun to see what that little rock could do with dandelion stained hands. It also could rub the skin right off with the stain.

8. In the case of plain old sour stomach from eating too much, a spoonful of bicarbonate of soda in a glass of water worked on that trapped gas under your ribs. Good work....Barf! Barf! Then you were ready for the piece of apple pie that you had just turned down.

9. Every cold I ever had ended up in a hacking cough, usually in the middle of the night. After I had coughed my head off for an hour and had awakened everyone in the house, my mother went into action. She went downstairs and brought in to the kitchen the little old oil stove for quick heat. She mixed molasses and butter and vinegar and sliced onions together. She would let it boil for a while. This syrup soothed the throat and stopped the cough much better than Smith Brothers cough drops ever did. Besides, it tasted pretty good, too. It may have been the beginning of sweet 'n' sour sauce over meatballs.

10. My grandmother George from Newfoundland rubbed a pink eye with a gold ring for 6 strokes. Pretty cool.

11. Rawleigh's Liniment. This was my mother-in-law's cure for everything, inside or out. That was

all right with me for the outside stuff like aches and pains in arms and legs. However, when she insisted it was the best cure for a cold, I dragged my feet. She wanted me to take a spoonful of this awful stuff and mix it with water. Finally, after ten years in the family, I figured it was now or never. When I got a sore throat, to keep on the good side of my mother-in-law, I did it. I swallowed some of this potion. It was the foulest tasting brew I ever had. I thought I was going to die. I didn't. And I never took it again. My mother-in-law? She kept right on taking it for the rest of her life and she lived to be 92 years old.

12. Balm of Gilead. Not one to complain about aches and pains and no patience to put up with any, Dad had his own cure-all. It was Balm of Gilead. This concoction made of large herb blossoms (I don't know what) saturated forever in rubbing alcohol, was good for sprains and charley horse and whatever. That glass jug had its own place in the corner of our bathroom ever since I could remember. Dad had to add more rubbing alcohol every 5 years to keep it going. The smell could knock you over when the cork stopper was off, but I guess that was part of the whole deal. My father claimed it did the job.

When it was my sad duty to "break up" my parents' home and I had to sort out all the keepers and the throw-always, I came across Dad's Balm of Gilead. I knew just what I was going to do with it. Whenever Dad had something that didn't work or was irritating, like a troublesome saltshaker, he would go out on the deck off the kitchen and fire that pesky saltshaker right into that little pond behind their house. The pond was very small and very deep and told no tales. As I stood on the deck holding the bottle of Balm of Gilead, I said, "This one's for you, Dad," and I fired it into the pond.

Clam Fritters...

1 cup flour
2 eggs
2 cups clam juice or milk
2 teaspoons baking powder

Remove black part of the clams
Chop clams
Mix all ingredients together

Drop from spoon onto hot greased pan.
Fry until golden brown.

Elsie Kimball
1935

Old Crow...

One Christmas when my dad and his sister Florence were in their eighties, my aunt gave Dad a bottle of Old Crow Whiskey. She claimed it would be good for his arthritis if he had a shot now and then. Dad didn't use it for that purpose because he had one of his own. That Old Crow got him the fastest oil delivery in town – the speed of lightning! Whenever Dad got a fill-up for his oil tank, he always gave that driver a slug of Old Crow. That delivery man kept our oil tank full all the time. With a come-on like that, how could Dad lose? And that driver? He was the happiest deliveryman in town. That Old Crow did more for that oil man than it would ever do for my father's arthritis.

Betty Kennedy Tufts

Spaghetti and Meat Balls...

Sauce

Fry 3 strips bacon until crisp.
Remove bacon from pan, leave the fat
Fry 3 cloves chopped garlic
2-3 onions
Handful of hamburg

Add to the pot...
Crumbled bacon
1 can tomato paste
1 can tomato sauce or tomatoes
Dash of cloves
Salt and Pepper
Let simmer

Meatballs

1 egg beaten
2 slices bread crumbled into egg
1 ½ lb. hamburg
1 chopped onion

Make into smallish ball
Dump into sauce.
Let simmer together 1-2 hours.

Mae Billings
1940

We Made Our Own Root Beer...

Every summer it was fun to make our own root beer. After we brought up the big canning kettle from the cellar, we scrubbed it to a fare-thee-well. We started with a bottle of Hires Root Beer Extract and we mixed in the required amount of sugar, When the sugar and extract mixed together was a chocolate color, it was time to add gallons of cold water. Sometimes when we were feeling a little wild we added extra hops to give it a big wallop. The odd bottle like ketchup or orange soda that we had saved from last year's batch of root beer were filled with our exotic brew and capped with our handy-dandy capper that everyone in the neighborhood borrowed, Then came that wonderful moment when we stored the new brew in the cellar beside our other canned goods.

We would have to wait at least two weeks for the root beer to work. One year we really got carried away with the hops and I guess we made this batch too potent. Soon after, in the middle of the night, we heard one pop after another. It was our root beer – one bottle after another exploding with the beat of Tchaikovsky's *1812 Overture*. That root beer had some authority this time! It went foaming all over the place with a very sticky sweet smell. Bad news. Our cellar smelled like a brewery all summer. And the other canned goods on the shelves with the root beer? The root beer covered everything. It clung to all the labels until they came sliding off. It made it pretty interesting all winter when we opened those cans - it could be canned corn or tomatoes. We never knew what we had until the cans were opened.

Cheese Cake...

Best of the Best

Crust
Mix...
¾ cup graham crackers crumbled
1 teaspoon sugar
1 tablespoon butter
Press into springform pan
Refrigerate until filling is ready

Filling
Soften before mixing
3 – 8 oz. pkg. Cream cheese
4 eggs
1 cup sugar
1 teaspoon vanilla
Beat like cream
Put into pan on top of crust
Bake at 350 degrees for 45 minutes

Topping
Mix...
2 cups sour cream
1 tablespoon sugar
1 teaspoon vanilla
Spoon over cake and bake at 350 degrees 5 or 10 minutes

Jean Kennedy
1968

Mel Learns to Drive

Everyone in town knew Mel Grant liked cars, but few people knew about his first one. It was a black open touring car that he had no idea how to drive. The year was 1925. Mel paid for the car and the dealer gave him the keys and said "Good Luck." Apparently driving lessons were not in the deal; Mel was strictly on his own. Not to worry. Mel figured he could operate that car soon enough. That very day, six family members; my aunt Florence with Mel, and my other aunts Ethel and Catherine and their husbands piled in on the heavy leather seats and set off in this sporty new automobile. There is a photo in my family of this trip; my aunts in gorgeous hats with scarves tied under their chins and my uncle in a straw boater. (Some class to the Irish.) Pulling knobs and working the clutch, after a jerky take off, Mel made it out of the driveway and onto the open road headed for Portsmouth no less. The saving grace of all this was Mel's was the only car on the road. Steering was no problem; it was the clutch that required a little attention. His passengers cheered him on in a cloud of dust. By the time they hit Portsmouth, Mel was a seasoned driver of some acclaim. After a bite to eat in Portsmouth and brushing off all the dust, they set out for North Berwick, reaching home late afternoon. Mel was a hero and as Lizzie Parker would say, "And a good time was had by all."

Betty Kennedy Tufts

Afternoon Tea Doughnuts…

Combine…
2 eggs beaten lightly
6 tablespoons sugar
¾ teaspoon salt
¼ teaspoon nutmeg
2 tablespoons melted shortening
6 tablespoons milk

Add…
2 cups flour
3 teaspoons baking powder
1 teaspoon vanilla
Mix well.

Drop by teaspoonful into deep hot fat.
Fry until brown.
Drain well and sprinkle with powdered sugar.

Ethel Kennedy Dunnells
Rebekah Cookbook
1930's

We'll Ride Up to Dover...

I spent a lot of time with my aunts and uncles. I loved to be with them and hear them talk. From my aunts it was the ordinary stuff like cooking and cleaning. They were altogether too neat and too clean. When one of them ran across a new cleaning product on the market, they all stood at attention to hear how it worked. And they were excellent cooks. I was lucky because I could stroll up one street and down another taking in all my aunts' good stuff. Fudge, raspberry turnovers, chocolate cake – it was usually at one place or another.

Now the uncles talked about baseball and Warren Spahn and what dogs made the best pets. They all concluded that it wasn't a cocker spaniel since my Uncle John's spaniel Toby went to the Vet's on a steady schedule because he picked up needles and pins.

My uncle had a lot to say when the State of Maine put VACATIONLAND on all the number plates. My Uncle Allie said, "Now how's that going to look on the plates of a hearse?" And they all thought he had a good point. They talked about their gardens. Dad preferred "pencil pod" string beans, my uncle liked "Jacob's Cattle." They all liked Katahdin potatoes. And the coffee my father liked was "Red Circle." My uncle Harland talked about hunting down around the quarry. Neat stuff to listen to.

Every Saturday night we went shopping in Dover, New Hampshire. That is, my mother and my aunts did the shopping. My father and uncle went to the movies and I got to go with them because I had acted so impatient while my mother was picking out a 25-cent card of buttons. She was so slow you could sing two verses of "Home On the Range" while she decided on the right ones. That was the last time for me. Good! She insisted I go with my father. I loved the movies with Laurel & Hardy, Wallace Beery and Marie Dressler in "Tugboat Annie". It almost blew it for me, though, when we went to see "Frankenstein." It didn't bother me that it was a little bit scary, but my mother had a fit. After that we were a little more careful and we didn't mention what movie we had seen.

After the movies we always ended up in Liggett's' Drug Store where I had hot chocolate with whipped cream on the top. With so many wonderful adventures, I loved those Saturday trips to Dover.

Betty Kennedy Tufts

Beef Casserole...

Place in buttered 13" by 9" casserole...
2 lbs. Beef cut in 2" chunks
1 cup red wine
1 onion sliced
1 cup sliced mushrooms
½ cup fine dry bread crumbs

Blend in a blender...
½ cup flour
1 10-½ oz. can beef consommé

Add to beef mixture
Salt to taste

Cover and bake at 300 degrees for 3-4 hours

Serve over noodle or rice.

For a hungry man!

Crochet, Knit, and Embroider…

Before the days of TV, folks sat around in the evening after the supper dishes were done and aprons were taken off and hung on the back of the pantry door. The men tuned in ballgames or the WEATHER. Weather had been the most talked about subject in Maine. In the old days when you were either a farmer or fisherman, it was necessary to plan around the storms and the frosts. And I guess it would always be that way for North Berwick people.

All our neighbors on Elm Street used the big cow weathervane on Mary Hurd's barn. They wanted to know what was ahead, though they couldn't do much about it, except pile up cord after cord of firewood.

Now women, on the other hand, had plenty of handwork to do. After darning and mending all the stuff that needed to be done, they could knit, crochet, braid, embroider or hook (rugs, I mean.)

I think most women liked to crochet. There were lots of projects to choose. If you were just starting out, you probably made a hot pot holder first. These holders were made in all different shapes with edges crocheted in a different color and a plastic ring sewed on the top to hang it. Those may have been the envy of everyone but me. I hated those because there were so many holes worked into the design that they exposed your hand to burns. More than once I howled to my mother to get rid of those, but she kept on hanging them up proudly. Things never changed. Those crocheted potholders were there to stay.

Then came chair back sets, one piece for each arm and a larger piece for the back. These were made to protect overstuffed lounge chairs. After that they became crocheted works of art. I remember a relative had a crocheted chair back that had a deer jumping in my direction and underneath it said, "Have a seat, my dear." (dear being the clue here.) In another household, there was a heavy crocheted rug in front of the bathroom door with WELCOME worked into the design. I don't think that was so bad because those trips to the bathroom might have been welcome indeed.

You see, there was a tremendous opportunity to be artfully original.

Embroidery was different. Pretty colors were used to make a design of fruits or flowers on linen "runners" for tables, pillowcases, or tablecloths. I saw a pair of pillowcases with "Good Night" embroidered in red on one and "Good Morning" on the other. That would go a long way to make your head ache if you slept on the wrong one.

These crocheters and embroiderers could never let things alone. They left their mark on everything from a knit dishcloth to a pink crocheted dress on a doll covering an extra roll of toilet paper. And I guess there's something to be said for that.

Betty Kennedy Tufts

Dumplings...

2 cups flour
4 teaspoons baking powder
½ teaspoon salt
2 teaspoons melted shortening
¾ cup milk

Mix quickly and drop by spoonfuls on top of a boiling stew
Keep well covered for 12 minutes.

Mason Jars and Vinegar...

Whenever women got together for a cup of tea or for a few minutes at noon hour at the mill, the subject of food and cooking usually came up and new recipes were swapped. A new way to can peaches or a different rule for making clam fritters was always an interesting challenge.

Most families in town had a garden every summer raising vegetables for the table and more than that, for CANNING. August and September were busy times for pickling and preserving. In our house every year we had a bushel of peaches to peel, slice, sugar and can. It was endless, fixing those peaches. I doubted I would ever eat one again. It was not my idea of a good time. And there were always cucumbers and peppers and onions to make mustard pickles, bread and butter pickles (Why did they ever call them that?) and piccalilli. Now there was a grind. After all that, it was time to work on the beans: string beans, all to be crammed into glass jars that had to be dragged up from the cellar and washed in soapy water to clean out the cobwebs. Then all those jars had to be so carefully placed in a big kettle to be boiled forever to sterilize them. If you didn't draw blood on one of those jagged tops, or you didn't suffer 3rd degree burns from fishing those jars out of the boiling water, you were home free.

After weeks of all this frenzy of canning and pickling, racing up the cellar stairs with the empty jars and then after all that work, carrying down the jars again after they were filled, peeling fruit, slicing cucumbers, I was fed up with the whole thing. Was all of this struggle worth a jar of chili sauce or shelled beans? I always thought Heinz did a pretty good job with pickles, myself. I complained about all this to my mother and four aunts one Sunday afternoon when they were sitting around all tired out after a week spent with all those jars and the vinegar. Well, I'll tell you it was like I had mowed down Mrs. Hurd's peonies next to the sidewalk. (Every year, Mrs. Spinney, wife of E.P. the judge, told me not to touch Mary Hurd's peonies as I walked by. She told me this every single year until I was old enough to vote.)

Tales of North Berwick

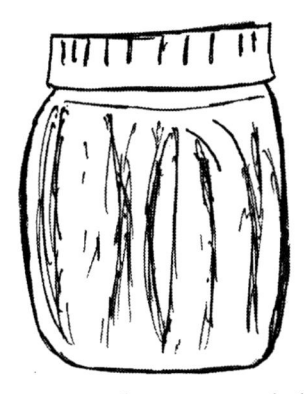

I mean, how much money did you save on a jar of peaches? Anyway, my aunts thought I'd never amount to anything, I guess. My aunts and my mother? They went right back at it the next day. Someone had told them how to pickle crab apples whole. Do you believe it? They were at it again, boiling, etc.etc.

Betty Kennedy Tufts

Potsfield Pickles...

Super!

Grind together...
3 lbs. green tomatoes
3 lbs. ripe tomatoes
3 red peppers
2 bunches celery
1 quart button onions
1 cabbage

Add...
½ cup salt and let stand over night. In the morning drain quite dry, as it makes more liquid as it cooks.

Add...
3 pints vinegar
3 lbs. sugar
½ teaspoon cinnamon
½ teaspoon cloves
½ cup white mustard seed

Cook 30 minutes.
Put into sterilized jars.
Seal immediately

Laura Tufts

Mustard Pickles...

Cut into small pieces the following and soak over night in a brine made of...
1 cup salt into 1-gallon water
1 quart small cukes
1 quart large cukes
1 quart green tomatoes (if you like)
1 quart button onions
1 cauliflower
3 or 4 green peppers

In the morning, bring the above to a boil in brine, which they soaked in. Drain. Now make the sauce.

Mix...
2 cups sugar (more if you would like)
1 cup flour
6 dessert spoons mustard (dry)
1 tablespoon turmeric

Mix all together with a little vinegar on stove and heat
Put 2 quarts vinegar on stove and heat.
Add the dry ingredients.
Mix all together well and add cut up pickles.
Mix together and heat thoroughly. Seal hot in sterilized jars closed tightly with jar rubbers.

This is the recipe my mother used. Can you imagine all that work?

Tripping the Light Fantastic…

North Berwick was a dancing town. It was 1915 and lots of young men in town would walk to wherever there was a place to kick up their heels. Of course, there was a dance at Commercial Hall now and then, but during the off Saturday night they went elsewhere. Maybe Sanford. Maybe Cape Porpoise, or Kennebunkport. Sometimes there were electric cars to take them part way. Their songs might be "Billy Boy," "Till We Meet Again," or "You Don't Know Nellie Like I Do,

Said the Saucy Little Bird on Nellie's Hat." Hard to dance to but it had a great message. Along with the music, which was usually a 3 or 4 piece band, the boys had plenty of hard cider on the side. Too much, sometimes.

There was the tale of Mellie Tobey, who lived on Maple Street. One night he had had his limit of hard cider and was quite unsteady on his feet. When he reached home he had a hard time making the front steps. The noise woke up his mother, who called out the window, "Is that you, Mellie?" Mellie replied, "Yes, Ma, it's me, and a tireder boy you never did see."

There was the tale of the fellas walking home from a dance in Sanford. They were almost home when one of them thought he needed some help getting there. He saw the tomb at the Hillside Cemetery and thought it was a house. He knocked and knocked on the door to see if the man of the house would give him a ride home. No luck, except it was a wonderful tale to tell on Monday morning.

Later on, dances were held in "The Little Hall" on the third floor upstairs of the building beside the bank. Those dances always featured the home town group, Syrena Chick, Ronnie Neal, and of course, Herbie Cole. The orchestra was small but they played great music. We heard "Loch Lomand," "Stardust," 'The Isle of Capri." Glenn Miller's boys couldn't have done it any better. We had some high old times in that little hall. Those dances attracted many young people from other towns.

ued
Sweet 'n' Sour Meatballs...

Combine...
1 2/3 lb. ground beef
2/3 cup cracker crumbs
1/2 cup chopped onion
2/3 cup milk
1 teaspoon seasoned salt
Mix lightly and thoroughly
Shape into about 30 meatballs
Place meatballs in a broiler pan and bake 20 minutes at 350 degrees.

Sweet 'n' Sour Sauce
Drain a 15 oz. size can pineapple chunks and save liquid.
Add water to pineapple syrup to make 1 cup and blend with 2 tablespoons cornstarch until smooth.
Stir in...
½ cup vinegar
1 cup brown sugar
2 tablespoons soy sauce
2 tablespoons lemon juice
1 cup chopped green pepper
½ cup maraschino cherries
Mix well and simmer for 15 minutes. Combine meatballs & sauce. This can be served over rice or alone in a buffet.

Spring Cleaning...

Every April in our town, SPRING CLEANING took over each household. Nothing was overlooked. Windows were thrown open, curtains taken down, rugs went on the clothesline, and every stick of furniture was polished. Boyle Brothers ran out of cleaning ammonia, vinegar (that was big in those days), Bon Ami, Fels Naphtha soap and laundry starch. I don't know how much cleaning the boys had to do, but the girls went into over-drive.

Armed with a skewer and orders from my mother, I had to dig out every corner of the windows with a mixture of ammonia and soap. Then the time came to take a cake of Bon Ami and load wet cloths heavily with it and go over all the window glass. When it was dry, we wiped off all the Bon Ami powder, leaving shiny clean glass and that white powder in all those corners I had just cleaned out with a skewer.

Now came the curtains. If they were lace, after they were washed they were stretched both ways onto a frame of long protruding tacks. The drill here was to put those curtains on those tacks without getting your fingers cut or bruised. It wasn't so much to cut your fingers as much as getting your blood all over the curtains. If you did, it meant that the curtains had to washed all over again and put through that sugar bath to stiffen the lace a bit.

Ruffled organdie curtains had their own schedule. After they were washed by hand, they were run through a stiff starch. Right here you had to know what you were doing when you cooked up that starch. It had to be boiled without any lumps. Blobs of starch wouldn't add too much to those ruffles. After the organdies were dried on the clothesline, they were sprinkled with warm water and rolled up until they were just right to iron. It seemed to me that those ruffles were miles long.

Rugs came next. In our house we had a big fat noisy Hoover vacuum cleaner. Dragging that Hoover around was like dragging a reluctant 10-year-old kid; it was so heavy. Sometimes it worked pretty good until tangled threads got caught up

Tales of North Berwick

in the brush underneath and it quit altogether. My mother waged a crusade against dust and dirt and I was her first sergeant. I cringed when I was told to "do" the dining room and living room. She meant I was to clean them but she thought to "do" them, didn't sound so much like work. Whatever. I hated this job when anybody could see those rooms were spotless anyway; I couldn't see a speck of dust anywhere. So my mother drew me into the hallway with a clear view of the dining room and she would say, "Just look at the dust on the sewing cabinet." Well, I did the cleaning. Not for long, though. I realized that if I kept that cabinet dusted off, the whole room looked just great, and I didn't need to do the rest. That worked for me until I left home in 1940. I never told my mother about this until she was 85 years old and I was 60. I figured I should confess, and not only that, what could she do to me now?

This spring-cleaning frenzy always took place during spring vacation, whether high school or college. It was planned then. It always makes me wonder when I see college students today on TV cavorting on the beach in Fort Lauderdale on their spring break, when two generations past they did their workouts in the clothes yard beating the daylights out of a parlor rug.

And so it goes.

Betty Kennedy Tufts

Cornflake Pudding...

3 cups cornflakes
1 quart milk
½ cup sugar
1 t4easpoon molasses
A piece of butter

Pour into a casserole pan
Set in a pan of water oven
Bake in slow oven for two hours

This recipe is so typical of the old ones – when did we use a quart of milk for one pudding? When did we bake a pudding for two hours?

Georgina Day
1929

And Then There Were These...

1. Mel Grant's Old English Bull Dog. His name was Peter. He resembled Winston Churchill except Pete drooled and Churchill didn't.

2. Al Kenney pulling that green wooden cart down Turkey Street. I never did know just where he went with it but I suppose he brought milk and cream to someone over town.

3. E.P. Spinney, lawyer and judge in our town. By his profession and his personality he was a cool and distant person. He was know by everyone as E.P., but always addressed as Mr. Spinney. I never heard anyone call him by his first name, Elvington. Right there is a clue.

4. Then there was John Chadbourne's gorgeous turquoise blue automobile. It was a <u>Cord</u> and none of us had seen the likes of it before! It was about 1936.

5. Earl Carter, Earl Thompson and Roger Bragdon…. buying and selling cattle around the countryside. The big 3 cattle dealers were all good friends. One of them said that if you wanted to make a deal anytime just pull out a wad of cash. No one could really resist the hard cash in hand.

6. Henry Vroom… Jim MacCorison's friend. He was always there to help Jim. Whenever he left the store, he would say, "I go now but I be back."

7. Geneva Neal Hobbs, Geneva was the musician in town. She was organist for the Congregational Church for a lifetime, I guess. She gave piano lessons to half the kids in town. She was a kind and gentle lady.

8. Ralph Staples' Bob Sled. I think Ralph's father, Clyde Staples, made the bobsled. Two wooden sleds joined together lengthwise with a long board running the entire length for a seat made this bob sled the best of them all. As many as 3 or 4 kids could ride. On the end was the boy who pushed the sled as hard as he could before he jumped on. The best ride was from the library on High Street, around the Old Corner, as far down as the bridge. Man! That sled was something.

9. Phil Dutch. Phil had a painting business. One time when he was painting the outside of our house on Elm Street, the nasturtiums were beginning to flourish in the little garden beside the porch. One morning when I went outside I was shocked to see all the big leaves were white! Phil had painted

Tales of North Berwick

them with white paint and tried to convince me they had bloomed overnight. I thought it was a hoot! What a great joke!

10. Christy Ford. Mrs. Ford was an elderly woman who had a dairy farm in Bauneg Beg. Once a week she'd drive down to the village in her Model A Ford. She carried butter in an old round wooden box with a wire handle. She made her sweet butter in squares with a fancy imprint on each quarter. Her butter was gently salted and just right. She had steady customers in town.

11. Harry Staples. Harry kept everyone guessing with his wit. Many tales were of Harry. Once when he was in Sanford driving his wagon with his old horse, the policeman put up his hand to tell him to stop. When Harry kept on going, the policeman blew his whistle at Harry and asked him why he didn't stop when he put his hand up. Harry said, "I thought you was waving at me." Another Harry Staples story: When his old horse died in the middle of the road, Harry scratched his head and said, "He never did that before."

12. Ronnie Neal. Ronnie, a flaming red head, was a musician but his best talent was his tenor voice. He sang in the church choir and had a hard time singing without grinning and laughing. He blushed a lot and laughed a lot. Ronnie liked everybody and everybody liked him.

13. Ollie Neal and Edla. Edla had a baking business in her kitchen, making cakes and cookies on

order from many in town. Ollie had a farm on High Street and raised a lot of vegetables, which he sold. Their younger son "Babe" (Oliver Neal, Jr.) rode all over town on his bicycle selling the produce. Babe graduated from the University of Maine and became a professor at the University of West Virginia. Even as a kid he loved botany. He usually had wooden stacks of pressed plants on their porch. The older brother Franklin,graduated from MIT and went with the Corning (NY) Company as a chemist.

14 .Staples Brothers Quartet. Walt, Clyde and Clarence Staples and Joe Gates, with great harmony performed for many events. Every-one enjoyed hearing them.

Apple Cake...

Cream...
1 cup sugar
½ cup butter
A pinch of salt
½ teaspoon of cloves
1 teaspoon of cinnamon
A pinch of nutmeg
1 cup raisins

Dissolve...
1 teaspoon soda in a little warm water.

Stir...
The mixture into 1 cup of stewed apples
Let it foam over ingredients in mixing bowl
Add 1 ¾ cups of flour

Bake 45 minutes at 350 degrees

Harriett Littlefield
Non Pareil Cookbook
1889

The Corset Lady…

The corset lady who sold corsets at house calls was on sacred duty when she arrived with a stout tape measure at your house. She meant business. After she measured you from top to bottom – and I do mean top and I do mean bottom, she made recommendations for just what you needed for good support and good form for a shape that had gone south. Not much was mentioned about comfort. That was the last thing she wanted to talk about. She showed several models of these garments and the choice was up to you. There was the kind that laced up the back. The lacings were good if you wanted no jiggle in the rear. Maybe you wanted the heavily boned number that shut down the circulation entirely, belted and buckled like the Wichita Lineman that Glenn Campbell used to sing about.

The tops of these corsets were engineered to lift bosoms that hadn't been lifted for twenty-five years. Ladies couldn't breathe very well in these and it was almost impossible to bend over, and a trip to the ladies' room was a challenge. But she was a vision. Every woman wearing one of these took on a haughty look. She was either convinced that she had the shape of Venus or she was in pain.

One day my mother and my aunts (all of them only size twelve and not needing corsets themselves) were talking about all the blessings of a certain corset. It seems that a young woman in our town, Anna, had one of these guaranteed firming up foundations. My aunt was sharing with her sisters what a marvelous shape Anna had now that she was laced in and boned up. They got carried away with Anna's invincible form. And then I said in a sarcastic tone, "Boy, I'll bet Willie likes <u>that</u>!"

And my aunts and my mother were appalled that I had said something so sexy. It was pretty bad of me, especially when that generation never would utter that word.

And that was sixty years ago.

Betty Kennedy Tufts

Red Cinnamon Apple Pie…

1/3 cup sugar
½ cup water
¼ cup red cinnamon candies
In saucepan, combine sugar, water and candies.
Simmer until candies are dissolved.

5 cups apples sliced for pie
3 tablespoons flour

Add…
Apples and flour to the candy mixture and
Cook until all is thickened.

Pour into pastry lined pan.
Bake at 375 degrees for 40 to 45 minutes.

From a New Hampshire Cookbook
1935

A Bell for Our Town…

The bell in the tower of the woolen mill rang every night on the hour from nine o'clock until seven in the morning. I don't know how many years this went on, but in the beginning it probably told time for the mill workers. You could set your Waltham by that bell. All well and good, the ringing of that bell could go either way. Most of us kids had better be home by the last peal of nine o'clock. Some times I thought that old mill bell had it in for kids. It always rang at the wrong time. When that bell rang at 9 PM, every kid in town (well, almost every kid) beat it for home, running or riding their bikes and if they were fast enough and they weren't too far away, they could make it home before that bell stopped ringing. Later when we went out on dates, it seemed to me that stupid bell started with its ungodly ringing when we were trying to sneak in quietly at an unlikely hour. Of course in those days, an ungodly hour was 12 o'clock. In the wintertime, when the snow was heavy and quiet, it was so comforting to hear that old bell.

Some of us remember the years when there was a piped-in program of carols played from the steeple of the Baptist church. Every evening before Christmas, we heard beautiful music coming over the crisp snowy air in our village. It felt good to be home.

Ruth Stillings' Baking Powder Biscuits...

2 cups flour
4 tablespoons Baking Powder
1 teaspoon salt
1 tablespoon lard
1 cup milk
1 tablespoon butter

Mix dry ingredients and sift twice.
Work in butter and lard with fingers.
Add liquid slowly, mixing with knife.
Toss on floured board.
Pat down and roll to ½" thickness.
Cut.
Put on greased baking sheet.
Bake 12-15 minutes at 425 degrees.

Ruth Stillings
1940

Shave and a Hair Cut…

Arthur Hooke's Barber Shop was like something out of Mayberry where Andy Griffith got his hair cut. Arthur's shop was upstairs over Charlie Goodwin's Candy Store and the Post Office. Tells you right there how important it was: there in the middle of downtown North Berwick. There was always plenty to see out of his windows, which had curved screens that provided almost three-dimensional view. Two windows faced the B & M railroad crossing where you could watch Ed Grant crank those gates up or down when a train was coming through. The other two windows faced the square and the North Berwick Bank so you could watch the crowds go in and out. I was very interested in that bank. I had a big savings account there, which was growing sluggishly. I usually banked the fifty-cent check from my uncle in New Brunswick every Christmas, and at two per cent you didn't need a prospectus to plot the growth of your account. But I kept hoping.

The bank was run? managed? by Mr. Campbell where he held forth on mortgages, auto loans and serious deposits. He ran a tight ship in that bank. I always felt like I had to curtsey when he waited on me. I felt his wrath many years later when I lost the key to our safety deposit box. He was really cranky that day. He stormed at me and said, "You just can not lose those keys!" And when I suggested that maybe he could give me another one, that was the end of a working relationship. I knew I could never float a loan at that bank.

Back to the barber shop. When my mother cut my hair I rebelled too much having her use the dull hand clippers over the back of my neck when those pesky hairs were yanked out one by one. She lost all patience with me and sent me to Mr. Hooke's barbershop where he took over my shingled hair do. It was like a Dutch cut, only clipped up the back It was all-the-go then. (Awful!) Well, it was a lucky break for me. That barber shop ranked right up there with Cliff Grant's smithy. It was a fascinating place, and the clientele were something, too. Whenever I went there for a shingle, there were always two or three men customers awaiting their turns for a shave or a haircut. We all sat around in those wooden armchairs with a spittoon in its own special place. On my first visit to the shop I had no idea what that spittoon was for until I saw one man draw back, pucker up, aim, and let sail a stream of tobacco juice through the air. You could actually hear it when it landed, mission accomplished. Then I could see his jaws working on more of the same: he was chewing tobacco (I had never seen that before) and getting ready to fire again. No one in the place seemed anxious that he would miss.

One of the customers asked me my name – remember this is a small town – and when I told him, he said, "Oh you're Frank Kennedy's girl!" And I was pegged right then and there; I was accepted into the brother-hood of the barbershop.

It was pretty interesting to hear these customers talk. They discussed today's weather, the government good or bad – depending on how you voted, their crops, or the weather predictions for the coming winter. All you needed to know. It was better than reading the <u>Portland Sunday Telegram.</u> Someone said, "Your potato crop doing good, George?" and George, (who was doing target practice on the spittoon) said he thought he'd get a good crop this year. Someone else might say " I wish the rain would hold off until I get my corn crop under cover, but I see that mackerel sky this morning and you know what that means. I think she's going to be a hard winter." They also talked about their cars and trucks, and in those days, it was usually about Fords and Chevys. Only Jim MacCorison had an Essex and it was green where everyone else's was red or blue. Takes a lot of tact to get along in a small town.

Then it was my turn in the barber's chair. First Arthur would put a board across the arms of the chair to raise me higher for my haircut. He put the apron over my clothes, plugged his electric shears into the one hanging cord from the ceiling and we were off! He asked me how I liked his barbershop. I sized up all those bottles and jars of his trade, the Bay Rum, all those fancy shaving mugs and especially the electric clippers. Those shears zipped right up my neck without a single yank. When he finished he used that nice soft brush to dust away all the stray hairs. I felt like a movie star, Claudette Colbert at least, having all that professional attention. I told Mr. Hooke I liked everything about it, a lucky break for me to be there.

Orange Sponge Cake…

2 eggs separated
1 cup sugar
1 orange juiced
Add cold water to the juice to equal ½ cup of liquid
1 ½ cups flour
1 ½ teaspoons baking powder
Beat together.

Pour into pan and bake at 350 degrees until edges on sides of cake come away from the pan.

Grace Howard
1935

The Hair Bob and Nail Polish...

It was the years of the flapper. The 1920's were big for the HAIR BOB. Women who had never before cut their hair now flocked to the hairdresser to have those long locks trimmed off up to the ears. Women now wore stylish "bobs" and let me tell you, those haircuts did a <u>lot</u> for some. Suddenly women who were long in the tooth became younger looking after half of the hair came off.

In our family my mother and her sisters all had their hair cut. I don't know about the others, but my mother saved all her long hair that had been cut off. Years later when I was looking for mittens on the closet shelf, I stuck my hands into a paper bag with all the hair. I was in shock. I thought an animal had made its home in our closet on Elm Street. After that I was inspired to use the hair for Halloween. That year I was a big hit as a witch

Tales of North Berwick

with all my mother's hair falling down around my face and hanging down the back from under that tall witch's hat. I put Black Jack gum on my front teeth and I was a shoo-in for first prize. My mother didn't see it that way. She felt I didn't show much respect for all that beautiful hair and right after that it disappeared.

These newly bobbed women did not stop there. Some of them had the new process for curling hair called the "permanent wave." The permanent started with all the women's wet hair parted off into strands and then wound around electric rods connected to a machine that fit like a helmet down over the head. And then the juice was turned on. How that electricity shooting through those hair rods made curls, I cannot imagine. It's a wonder all these women lived through it, and at least, weren't all bald. When the rods were taken off, those heads were covered with rolls of hair like grade A large sausages. The wave set helped a lot to smooth things down into a crimped hair do. Amazing.

About that time there was a popular hairdresser in North Berwick who "did" the hair of every one of her customers the same identical way, part-by-part and wave-by-wave with the little hank of hair on the forehead. It didn't make any difference, young or old. It was sort of startling at church or graduation to see every woman there looking the same. No imagination there. Even the girls in the high school graduation class having their hair "done" for the first time looked just like their grandmothers, their mothers and all the aunts in the front row. Not even Mary Kay could pull that off. Those young girls with that hairdo looked older than God – or at least twenty years older than the 18 they were.

Colored nail polish was something else. At first it caused quite a stir. It came out in all shades, fire cracker, poppy, scarlet, cranberry, or mauve. In the beginning, only the movie stars used it and then only the "fast" girls went for it until it caught on for all. With dark red polish on my fingernails all I could see were ten fingers with tips that looked like ten kidney beans.

Women in our town set a fast pace for beauty.

Baked Rice Pudding…

1 quart milk
1 cup of rice
½ teaspoon salt

Combine and bring to a boil.
Add…
¾ cup sugar
2 eggs well beaten
2 cups Half and Half
Pour into a greased casserole dish.
Bake in 350-degree oven for an hour.

Food Sales and Cookbooks...

We all know the story of Berwick Sponge Cake. Early on, when the train stopped in North Berwick, the passengers would enjoy refreshments...sponge cake. The cake was so good; it became famous.

Beyond that, North Berwick cooks were never topped, and good food was used to make money. One way was to have a food sale held in a local store. This was where cooks showed off their best baking. My mother's specialty was brambles, a 2-crust pastry square filled with nuts and raisins. Stella Swett made the best chocolate cake and Blanche Hamilton's daffodil cake was popular, too.

Another moneymaker was the sale of cookbooks featuring the best recipes in the outfit; maybe the Rebekahs or the Grange or the WCTU, which was Womens' Christian Temperance Union fighting

John Barleycorn. We liked Pearl Lincoln's divinity fudge and Laura Hardy's orange sponge cake in the Rebekahs' book. Everyone had a chance for a moment of glory when her recipes were chosen, but no one could make a better oyster stew than the men did at the Masonic Hall.

Cooking has changed since then. Right here I want to say I miss the vegetables and the way they were cooked before Tex-Mex, Salsa and zucchini took over our New England way of life. Those heavy-duty spices spoil all the taste of the real veggie for me. No one can make ordinary American Chop Suey any more without loading it with garlic and chili powder. Even plain old buttered mashed potatoes are different. To start with, they pass up Katahdin potatoes for the Yukon Gold, they add chicken bouillon to it and it isn't mashed potatoes, as we know it. Terrible! Or fried potatoes now – they cook them up with diced onions and paprika. Mashed potatoes; they were special with lots of butter and whipped up with cream. They were some good. I heard the story where Laura Hardy was demoted from mashed potato duty to butter cutter at the annual Congregational Harvest supper in 1939 because she put cold milk into the potatoes. And that, my friends, was not the way it was done. Only hot milk made them fluffy.

Back to the vegetables. Take zucchini; (please!) we could do without it. In the last 50 years zucchini has taken over every backyard garden. People plant it because it grows so well and then they don't know what to do with all of it and they give it to each other and finally in desperation to use it up, they put it in bread, cake and cookies. (I was just happy with brown sugar in my cookies.) It has also flooded the restaurant market. On the menu, they call it vegetable medley, but don't let them fool you. It's always zucchini. No matter how pricey or how cheap – every restaurant throws it on every plate with slices of summer squash; and it's never cooked enough. Whatever happened to ordinary peas and carrots with a good steak?

Give me plain old vegetables; cooked enough so you don't need a knife to cut them up after you chase them all over the plate. And of course, always real butter and real cream on all of them, I'll take those, and new generations can keep the salsa, garlic, chili powder and half cooked veggies.

Brambles…

Raisins Mixture
1 cup seeded raisins (the kind with the seeds in)
1 cup sugar
1 egg
½ teaspoon salt
Grind up raisins
Add…
1-cup sugar
1 egg
½ Teaspoon salt
Cook slowly until thickened. Cool before pouring over pastry. Chopped walnuts may be added.

2 cups pie crust mix
Combine pastry with cold water to make dough. Divide into 2 parts. Roll one portion into a large rectangle sheet to fit cookie sheet. Spread with cooled raisin mixture. Roll out other pastry for the top.
Place on top of the raisins.
Turn over a bit of lower crust up over the top crust. Flute edge.
My Mother's Recipe
1930
She always made these for food sales.

The Pharmacist and The Soda Man...

On the ground floor of Commercial Hall, the owner, Richard Hurd, had a drug store. A pharmacist, he filled prescriptions and made his own medicines as well. He was known for his *Nervine* pills for the nerves and *Smashine* pills to fight colds. He was a smallish man, very dapper, with glasses perched on his nose and ready to grind up a new medicine.

Hurd's Drug Store also sold ice cream and soda at the marble counter with wire stools to perch on. Second in command at the store was John Plaisted, a big kindly man who mixed up the sodas, sundaes, and phosphates and scooped the ice cream cones. Mr. Hurd was known to be snug when dipping out the Fro-Joy ice cream or putting it into the box, but you could always get a more generous scoop from Mr. Plaisted. Whenever we found Mr. Plaisted busy, we shuffled around the corner until he was free to wait on us. It was always disappointing when Dick Hurd took up the ice cream scoop and did the dipping. Mr. Hurd and Mr. Plaisted ran the drug store...each in his own way.

Hurd's Drug Store seemed dark and dismal to me. They sold newspapers and magazines and all kinds of medicines and drugs. On the shelves were iodine, camphor, Vapo-Rub, True's Elixer and Castoria for a laxative. It was about that time that someone thought the word physic was a little crude, so the delicate word for it became laxative. It's all how you look at it I guess. Hurd's sold cod liver oil. No capsules here, just that oil right off a teaspoon every day. But none of it was as bad as castor oil. That was the heavy duty stuff. Guaranteed!

The drug store also sold Kodak film for cameras and then sent it to Portland to be developed. Not only that, they sold reserved seats for all the drama productions in Commercial Hall upstairs.

On the right hand side of the store were glass cases of medical supplies: crutches and canes, bed pans, and arm slings. They must have been displayed there forever because I never saw anyone buying any of that stuff. Shows right there how tough North Berwick people were, because they didn't need any of those supplies.

You could say that Hurd's Drug Store had it all, coming and going.

The Perfect Hand Lotion...

Boil slowly for 2 hours...
1 oz. quince seed
1 qt. Water

Strain through cheesecloth and cool

Add...
1 oz. rose water
1 oz. glycerin
1 oz. Listerine
2 tablespoons alcohol
10-cents worth of tincture of benzoine

Add...
2 tablespoons of toilet water for perfume

Mix well and bottle.
Makes one quart.

Maine Rebekahs Cookbook
1930's

Boyle Brothers Store...

On the other side of the Commercial Block, on the ground floor was Boyle Brothers Grocery Store. The store was owned by Charlie and Dave Boyle with Timmy Johnson as hired help. It was a dark and dreary place like most grocery stores then. When you went to their store to buy, you stood at the front counter and waited with your list while Timmy fetched and carried. It was no day at the beach for Timmy; it was a workout, traveling all over that store to fill the orders. Timmy was a gentle, shy man who lived on Turkey Street with his two sisters; Maude, who worked at the bank, and Sarah, who kept house for all of them.

Every night after work, Timmy picked up Maude at the bank and drove home in his black model A Ford with the green spoke wheels and a painted tin cutout "Maine" on the radiator. Those were the days of exposed radiators on cars; none of the fancy hoods like we have today on our Chryslers. That tin shape of the state of Maine was Timmy's vanity plate of 1930s.

The reason I can recall Timmy's car so well is that I rode all over the countryside with Tim and my Dad decorating veterans' graves on Memorial Day. We did it every year. Tim and Dad had a map of North Berwick in which someone had documented the graves of veterans in our town. Most of them were in the two big cemeteries, but some of them were at the end of a country road, some on the home place of a crumbling farmhouse. It was a good lesson for a child. I learned that all war veterans of our land should be recognized, whether in a town plot or in the woods of another time. Each grave had a new flag every year and a salute from two of their own, Timmy and Dad.

Back to the store. When Timmy finished filling an order, he added it all up with his pencil on a brown paper bag, and he was always right. Charlie made house calls every week to his customers, taking orders for delivery the last of the week. He also delivered all the news of the town. In those days, ordering groceries was easier than it is today. In a grocery store today, there are thirty-nine kinds of soap, twenty kinds of cereal, ten kinds of bread, and fifteen kinds of shortening. Back then it was Ivory or Fels Naptha soap, cornflakes or shredded wheat, white or raisin bread, and one kind of shortening…lard. Today it takes a college education to pick out peanut butter; crunchy, super crunchy, creamy, cheap (the kind you have to stir in the oil,) Jif, Skippy, Peter Pan, or the kind that just says <u>Peanut Butter.</u> I don't buy that kind, it seems suspicious to me when the manufacturer won't put his name on the product.

Charlie's wife, Evie, was the leading soprano in the choir of the Congregational Church. She was known to hit all the high notes with remarkable force, balanced by Lewie Guptill, basso profundo of great proportions himself. It was worth it to show up at church on Sunday morning just to take in their unplanned duet. Evie was also the only woman in town with purple shoes. Now there is something to set a woman apart from the crowd.

Charlie and Dave ran a good store. They were honest, kind, fair and friendly. Good people all of them.

Tales of North Berwick

Don't Worry's Hermits...

1-½ cups sugar
2 teaspoons cream of tartar
2/3 cup butter
1 cup chopped raisins
2 eggs
½ teaspoon cloves
¼ cup milk
½ teaspoon cinnamon
3 ½ cups flour
½ teaspoon nutmeg
1 teaspoon soda
1 cup chopped nuts
¼ cup molasses

Cream...
Butter and Sugar
Beat eggs and add to milk
Stir into sugar and butter
Add four, spices…. nuts last.

Place in greased pan
Bake at 350

65 years ago, The Boston Globe ran a page of Confidential Chat of letters and recipes signed with pen names. This recipe was from "Don't Worry" Sometimes two women with pen names carried on a friendship in the newspaper for many years. In 1957 when I was in Concord, N.H., I made a friend who told me that she had written to Confidential Chat as "Cranberry Cove." My

mother had read Cranberry Cove's letters and recipes for several years.

Parcel Post or RFD...

Our post office in North Berwick was little more than a hole-in-the-wall wedged between Goodwin's Candy Store on the left and Wilfred Snow's Store on the right. I never knew what Wilfred sold in his little store, but it must have been something because he wouldn't keep paying rent and electric light bills in that place unless he sold something. And whatever it was, he kept at it for lo, these many years.

Leonard Meader was postmaster for a long time. The sameness of all those mailboxes or cubbies must have dampened his sense of humor because he didn't laugh much. And if you get right down to it, laughter never got the mail out on time. I was always a bit nervous when I asked for a 3-cent stamp. I felt I was snubbing the United

States Postal Service with only a three-cent run of business. I'm sure the rural free delivery men didn't feel much like telling jokes either, when they were loading their delivery trucks. Actually these old trucks belonged to the men, not the USPS. They only put the sign on their trucks when they were delivering mail. There was always business for these men; noisy baby chicks, or a shipment of Sears Roebuck catalogs. Those babies were heavy.

Back to Len Meader, he did have one amazing talent. He could add a column of figures faster than an adding machine. Now how spectacular is that? Can you do it?

Clarence Staples was the next post-master. He waited on me for stamps or a money order with a chuckle because he called me "Gloomy." That was because I laughed so much. My greatest problem in life so far was seeing something funny when the humor escaped my parents. I paid for it every time.

After I went away to school, on my letters home, I often wrote "Hi Clarence, it's Gloomy" on the back flap. After a while my father said, "Who is this Gloomy person on the back of your mother's letters?" It was a jokey thing for a year or two. Clarence liked that. He and I were good friends.

The mail was put up several times a day after the trains came in. The latest one was seven o'clock in the evening when the post office was still open. It was a handy excuse for us to get out after supper to see our boyfriends who were not far away at the time, waiting at the end of the street. We just said we were expecting something in the mail for English class. Now what could that possibly be? It sure wasn't Shakespeare sending me something by parcel post. What a dumb alibi. But it worked every time! I wonder how many of us ever got to the 7 o'clock mail or how many parents believed us.

Betty Kennedy Tufts

Walnut Strips...

Mix together…
½ stick butter
½ cup flour
Press into 8" x 8" pan
Bake at 350 degrees for 12-15 minutes
Mix together…
1 egg well beaten
¾ cup light brown sugar
1 tablespoon flour
¼ teaspoon salt
1/8 teaspoon baking powder
½ cup chopped walnuts
1 teaspoon vanilla
Put on baked crust
Bake for 15-20 minutes at 350 degrees

Icing
1 1/2 tablespoons butter
1 cup frosting sugar
1 tablespoon orange juice
1 ½ teaspoon lemon juice
Top icing with chopped walnuts.

I don't know where this recipe came from, but I do remember eating these for the first time at a Valentine's Day tea party in 1968. I wrote the recipe down then.

Ice Cream and Fireworks…

Charlie Goodwin's store next to the post office had a soda fountain where he sold his own ice cream. He made it in the backroom of the store. Charlie's and later his son Orville's ice cream was an acquired taste. All the kids loved it because it was sweeter and creamier than Hood's or Fro-Joy. It also came in some grand colors. My favorite was strawberry because it was shocking pink, just the color of bubble gum. They also made molasses sponge candy that quickly dissolved in your mouth, cornballs, and candy kisses called Goodwin's Puffs. Later Orville took over the store and Mabel Bragdon tended the penny candy case. There were wax whistles, green and white pieces, walnut squirrels, hot balls and licorice ropes. They also had a tray of spruce gum; each was wrapped in brown paper. It really tasted awful but none of us ever admitted it and kept right on chomping it, working hard to soften it up. Mabel was very patient with us, standing on one foot and then the other, while we made our choices.

And Goodwin's store sold fireworks for the glorious Fourth of July. Every year before Independence Day, Orville put out an exciting spread of fireworks in his front window. Kids cashed in soda bottles (not the ones kept for root beer making) to get the cash to buy those wonderful Roman candles, sparklers, sky-rockets, and little Chinese firecrackers. If you felt really daring you set off all of the fire-crackers at one time. And, of course, there were the big time 5 inchers. We took a lot of time standing at that window planning how we would spend our money.

On the day of the glorious Fourth, we could hear firecrackers and whistlers and any kind of noisemaker all over town. Kids hoarded their own supply and once in a while traded, if they thought they could make a bigger noise or better display.

In the evening it was customary for our family of aunts, uncles, and cousins to go to our grandparents' home on Elm Street and put all our fireworks together to make a really big extravaganza. One year my 5-year-old cousin

Johnny got carried away by all the excitement and moved too close to the sparklers. He became a sparkler himself when his pants caught on fire. Johnny's pants made a good showing of fireworks that we hadn't planned on. Wow! Talk about explosions. The explosion of all my aunts was louder than any 5-inch firecracker we had. They got the fire on his pants put out quickly. Johnny suffered no bad results except he spent the rest of the festivities in his Fruit-of-the-Loom underwear.

The adults set off the skyrockets and aimed them to shoot out over Mary Hurd's pasture. Those skyrockets probably scared those Holsteins out of three days' worth of milk and cream.

It was a gala night of great happenings in our little town in York County.

Betty Kennedy Tufts

Norwegian Apple Pie...

¾ cup sugar
½ cup flour
1 egg
1 cup diced apples
½ teaspoon vanilla
¼ teaspoon salt
1 teaspoon baking powder
½ cup chopped walnuts

Combine dry ingredients
Beat in egg and vanilla
Add nuts and apples

Bake in buttered pie pan for 30 minutes at 350 degrees

Serve with whipped cream

Cookbook
1930's

Norwegian Macaroons...

Combine and mix well...
1 cup butter
2 cups sugar
1 cup oatmeal
1 cup coconut
2 eggs well beaten
1 teaspoon almond extract

Add...
2 ½ cups flour
¼ teaspoon salt
1 teaspoon baking powder
½ teaspoon soda

Roll into small balls and then into sugar
Place balls on a greased cookie sheet.
Bake at 350 degrees for 10 minutes

The cookies may be topped with a cherry half before baking.

Makes about 60 cookies.

From an old cookbook 1930's
These are so good!

The Great Atlantic and Pacific …

The local A & P store was run by Bill Matthews. He stocked all the A & P groceries; but what interested me the most was the A & P cookies sold in bulk. They were the ones with a fat marshmallow top covered with shredded coconut on a chocolate cookie. They were kept in a metal case with a glass top that we lifted up; and we loved to fish them out, one at a time. It was fun to break the cookie away from the marshmallow when we could lap out the dab of phony raspberry jam underneath, then chew the coconut. At school during recess, there were swaps between the wholesome molasses cookies brought from home and the sticky A & P kind that all the kids loved.

Frank Matthews, known to us as "Hot Dog," worked for Mr. Matthews. He put on that big white apron, and later became the manager of the store. Hot Dog always beamed with a wide grin. Everyone was fond of Hot Dog and liked to visit the store just to see him inside that always smelled of freshly ground coffee, either Bokar or Red Circle.

Betty Kennedy Tufts

Favorite Ginger Snaps…

Mix together…
½ cup soft shortening
1 cup sugar

Stir in…
1 cup molasses
½ cup water

Add…
4 cups flour
1 teaspoon soda
1 ½ teaspoons ginger
½ teaspoons cloves
½ teaspoons nutmeg
¼ teaspoons allspice

Mix all together and chill
Form balls then dip balls in sugar
Place balls on a cookie sheet
Press each ball with bottom of a glass to form cookie.
Bake in a 375-degree oven until crisp
Very old recipe

J.O. MacCorison, Mr. North Berwick...

Jim ran a men's clothing store across the street from the Commercial Block. He also served as town clerk and Justice of the Peace. He sold real estate and wrote insurance policies. Jim was very popular, affable, caring and most of all, good natured and funny. I remember Jim owned a dark green Essex automobile with the square box corners on the back. That Essex was always parked in front of his store, ready to roll.

Jim's father was Doctor Mac Corison, a real country doctor who rode to his patients in his horse and buggy. Jim and his brother Jack were pals of my father when they were kids and they ran together all over town. Dad told the story about Jim and his new dog "Hunka." Jim's mother, a sweet lovely lady, said "Jimmy, that is a strange name for a dog." What Jim never told his mother was that the dog's real name was "Hunka S___!"

After Dad and Jim served in the Armed Forces during WWI, they were still pals. They were very active in veterans' affairs and helped many of the "boys" establish their records for disability and military pensions. Everyone in our town liked Jim and respected him as well. He was a favorite.

Maine Shrimp Casserole

8 slices of bread, buttered and cubed
½ pound sharp cheese cut up fine
2 cups cooked Maine shrimp
3 eggs well beaten
2-½ cups milk
½ teaspoon salt

Alternate layers of bread cube, cheese and shrimp starting with bread cubes in a buttered casserole.
Beat eggs well
Add milk and salt
Mix well and turn over content of casserole
Bake one hour at 325 degrees

1940

Cherry Cake...

1-cup sugar
½ cup shortening
2 eggs beaten lightly
¾ cup milk (scant)
1 small bottle maraschino cherries cut up...save liquid
2 cups flour
½ teaspoon salt
2 even teaspoons baking powder
Cream thoroughly...
Sugar and shortening
Add...
Eggs and beat well
Add...
Cut up cherries
Part of liquid in bottle and the milk
And then dry ingredients
Sift flour and baking powder 3 times
Bake in moderate oven

Frosting
1 ½ cups confectioner's sugar
1 tablespoon butter
Cream butter and sugar
Add remaining cherry liquid until frosting is ready to spread.
Beat well.

Gertrude Welch

North Berwick and the B & M...

Our town was a center for the Boston and Maine Railroad, having both divisions coming through. North Berwick was on the way from Boston to all points in Maine. The depot was beside the center of our town with its stores and bank. Before the first set of tracks was the gatehouse and the ever-watchful Ed Grant, the portly gatekeeper. He raised and lowered the gates manually whenever the trains came through. Those were the days of the majestic, powerful steam locomotive with the huge round light on the front, like a king-sized belly button. The trains made 5 or 6 stops a day for passengers, mail and baggage. The woolen mill shipped out huge rolls of woolen cloth wrapped in brown paper bound for New York on the afternoon train.

Inside the station were the ticket office and the waiting room. There were long varnished wooden benches with backs of punched out holes in the design "B & M." Pretty swell. The floor was old dingy, oiled wood. On the sides of the waiting room were ugly radiators that took on a life of their own in cold weather, clanging and knocking loudly. No frills or decorations here, just a garish, printed calendar of a pretty girl in a Jantzen bathing suit drinking Moxie.

The baggage master was Frank McCrillis, a giant of a man with a very loud commanding voice to match. He met the passenger trains with a big 4-wheel green painted handcart to unload boxes and crates. Sometimes it would be steel parts of machines tagged for the mill, or there would be crates of peeping chickens headed for local farmers. And then came the war years of the 1940s when Frank unloaded the coffins of local boys who were casualties of the wars in Europe or the Pacific. Frank always handled these with extra care and deep respect. Frank could do it all.

Al Eaton was a conductor for the Boston and Maine passenger cars. He was a short, round, jolly man. He wore his official black suit with the brass buttons and the cap that hardly covered the curly fringe of hair beneath it. He was a very friendly good man who went to the Congregational Church in town. He knew I sang in the choir. Whenever I boarded the train for a trip to Boston or Portland, I ducked down in my seat so he wouldn't notice me. If he saw me he would say "Just one chorus of *Brighten The Corner Where You Are*, Betty." Right there in that passenger car, I didn't want to sing and I didn't want to brighten any corner wherever I was – especially on that train!

Sometimes I went down to the station with my classmate, Eula Brooks, to meet her dad who was an engineer for one of the trains. Once when he was there with some of the cars uncoupled, he asked us to come aboard the locomotive and sit in the engineer's seat while he took the engine down the tracks a mile or two and then back again. We were thrilled! Two eleven-year-old girls running the train (we thought) and blowing the whistle. Can you beat that? All we needed were blue and white engineer's caps.

Freight trains sped over the tracks in the village. We used to count the cars all the way to the end of the caboose. There were cars from all over the country. Painted on the sides were B & M, Bangor and Aroostook, Lackawanna and Lake Erie. Sometimes we counted 75 cars. During the war years the trains were made up of many more cars sometimes and they seemed to run in darkness of the night.

When WWII was over, so many passenger cars were not needed to transport troops. Then came "The Flying Yankee," silver and streamlined, which took the place of steam locomotives; but never did they have the presence of the fascinating sound of the steam train whistle in the night when it passed Varney's Crossing.

Salmon Loaf…

Soak 18 saltines in 1 cup milk
Add…
Juice from one can of salmon
½ cup evaporated milk

Add…
2 teaspoons grated onion
2 tablespoons melted butter
2 eggs beaten
1 can of boned salmon
 Cook in a mold set in water in 350 degree oven

Onion Sauce

Sauté…
1 large sliced onion
1 stick butter
Sauté until onion slices are transparent.

Ladle over cooked salmon loaf when serving.

Wonderful!
1947

Current Events...

Every school, including ours, spent time on Current Events. Most of our news came from newspapers and the radio. For some kids hearing about the news was mostly in school. In the 20's, we had just gotten over World War I and adjusting to peace. Boys in our school wore leatherette helmets with flaps down over the ears and sporting goggles; they were aces. Remember these were the 20's and the early days of aviation. Boys loved it.

Then in 1929 came the Stock Market Crash. It was hard for grade school kids to understand, but then they did realize the hard times the Depression meant. During the 20's it was very common to hear about North Berwick folks who had moved to the city for good jobs, now found no work there. These North Berwick people moved back home where there was always food from gardens and fuel for heat; North Berwick was a much kinder place to be during those days.

During the hard times of the Depression many men walked from town to town and state to state looking for work. They existed on the food passed out to them by townspeople wherever they happened to be. Our house was on both Routes 4 and 9 and many tramps came by. My mother, when my father was home, fixed up a meal for the men who knocked on the door. Dad always sat on the porch with these men and heard many interesting and sad stories. Sometimes these hobos found overnight shelter in the old firehouse on Portland Street, called the "lock-up." We almost never had a lawbreaker in this place and the tramps were grateful for the shelter in their travels.

I don't remember that we kids realized how tough times were then. The only inconvenience that came my way was discontinuing piano lessons that I was getting from Geneva Hobbs. Secretly I was tickled to death, as I hated all that practicing. I felt lucky that I could quit.

Then in 1936, we learned about Civil War in Spain. It didn't mean much to me until the movie "For Whom the Bell Tolls" came out. Gary Cooper and Ingrid Bergman starred as fighters for the Cause, living in caves and blowing up bridges.

I will never forget that scene nearly at the end of the movie when Gary Cooper was wounded so badly that the other fighters had to leave him there under an olive tree. (I guess it was an olive tree – those olives were big over there.) Their chief guerilla kissed Gary on both cheeks, stood up tall, saluted him and said "Salud, Roberto." (That was Cooper's name in the movie.) I loved that line "Salud Roberto" and it comes in handy when I meet someone named Robert. Only once in a while does someone know what I'm talking about. It's far more interesting to say "Salud Roberto" than it is to say "Hi Robert."

I also loved the haircut Bergman wore; short and curly – they call it unstructured today. But when I had the Bergman haircut, no one ever said I looked like Maria except for a freshman boy in Civics class who was trying to impress me. But I did love the look.

After Silent Cal and Herbert Hoover, the country was ready for FDR. We learned about CCC, WPA, and PWA. College kids used NYA, National Youth Administration to pay their tuition. They got $.35 an hour working on campus and were glad for it. In a town like North Berwick where the whole economy depended on the woolen mill that ran only now and then, many citizens were grateful for Franklin Roosevelt's new programs.

Out of work, artists found jobs in these government plans. They painted murals decorating post offices and other federal buildings. Sometimes this art was not appreciated by those natives whose only art experience up until then, were paintings of roses in a vase and moonlight on the ocean. These people in coastal Maine did not like murals picturing naked kids and fat ladies in bathing suits on Kennebunk Beach pictured in their Post Offices. People protested sometimes but it really did broaden their ideas of art.

Our country went to war again in 1941 and everyone was in it, one way or the other. I was in college by then and several friends and I took courses and became Air Raid Wardens for the State of Maine. I still carry that ID card in my wallet. Doesn't mean a thing, but I've kept it anyway, along with my card from Massachusetts that gives my blood type. Either way, I'm prepared. I don't know why we thought a little town like Gorham with its small college would ever be any threat to Japan or Germany. I can't imagine Gorham would be a target for the Third Reich, but we were ready with our flashlights.

In North Berwick, citizens manned the Air Civil Defense towers in High Pine and Wells

Beach. They took turns watching for enemy aircraft. The towers were along the coast of Maine and performed great service for defense.

We sang "I left My Heart at the Stage Door Canteen," "Good Bye, Dear, I'll Be Back in a Year (they weren't), "There'll be Blue Birds Over the White Cliffs of Dover," "Praise the Lord, and Pass the Ammunition," "Don't Sit Under the Apple Tree with Anyone Else But Me," (the next line was "till I come marching home") "Coming In on a Wing and a Prayer." I am not making these up; they were all popular songs during WWII.

North Berwick sent many young people to war, and we lost many who didn't come home. People had different ways of showing their loyalty and their grief. Some were insensitive and off the wall. When one soldier from our town was lost in a sad action, my father offered condolences to the young man's father-in-law. This man thanked Dad for his sympathy and then he said, "I really don't know what we are going to do without him – he was the best poker player we had."

It was a time of hardship and worry until 1945 when peace was declared. Then North Berwick had to face up to healing and our town did well. We were all in it together.

Mushroom Sandwich...

Saute...
1 cup fresh sliced mushrooms in
2 tablespoons butter
Add...
½ tablespoon flour
2 tablespoons of cream
½ beef bouillon cube

Stir it all up
Put mushroom mixture into buttered bread
Then grill the sandwiches.
Makes two sandwiches.

This came from an old friend
in N.H.
1960's

Betty Kennedy Tufts

Downeast Blueberry Cobbler…

Mix together in large sauce pan…
2/3 cup sugar
2 tablespoons corn starch
Add ¾ cup water.
Boil for 1 minute stirring constantly
Add…
3 cups of fresh or frozen blueberries
Heat all together and
Pour into 9" pie pan
Top with…
1 teaspoon cooking oil
1 teaspoon cinnamon

Topping
1 cup flour
1 ½ teaspoons baking powder
½ salt
Mix with…
½ cup milk and 3 tablespoons oil
Stir together and drop by spoonfuls onto blueberries
Bake at 425 degrees for 25-30 minutes

Every Maine cook always had a favorite blueberry dish. This is mine.

Hillside...

There is one thing about a cemetery that I don't understand. I mean the cemetery that has a fence around it. What good is that fence anyway? Who needs it? People inside can't get out and the people outside don't want to get in.

A walk through Hillside Cemetery is like a visit with old friends and family. I noticed the grave of a young North Berwick boy, Edward White, a gunner on a "flying fortress", one of those huge bombers in WWII. He was lost in 1944 when his plane went down in the English Channel. The plane, after dropping its load of bombs over Germany, was riddled with direct hits and never made it back. He is not in this grave; only a gravestone is there to say that he had lived; a boy who never came home.

Some of the older graves mark the places of WWI veterans. I remember as a child seeing those men wearing their old uniforms, ill fitting now, but proud in the Memorial Day parade. These men got fewer and fewer and couldn't march anymore, and so they rode in an open car in the parade. Then came along the veterans of WWII to take their places in the parade and later in the cemetery.

I notice the grave of an old school friend, a North Berwick young man who died in a prison camp in Germany in 1943. He and I were partners in the chemistry lab in high school. I loved being his partner because he could think of the strangest things to do with the experiments. Elroy was so smart he made up new results of the experiments. He made them look so good he talked his way through it with Mr. Cobb, who made everyone else change their results (which were valid) to agree with Elroy. I shook my head and laughed every time.

Elroy always signed his name on assignments, reports, exams and papers with an ESQ. after his name, Elroy Wyman. He explained that ESQ. meant he was a landowner. He was remarkable for his trading; trading up every time until he ended up owning a boat or a piece of property, starting with an old bike that he had shined up. I always felt he would have gone on, had he lived, to owning all the rivers and half the town.

Tales of North Berwick

There was one corner of the cemetery having graves with simple metal markers. They were the graves of the unknown or those who had no family and those who came from who knows where. One of these markers showed the grave of Bill Gallagher who was the "hired man" of a farm family in Bauneg Beg. Whenever my uncle cared for the graves of my grandparents, he always went over and mowed old Bill's grave and sometimes left a flower. He had known Bill who had worked on the Billings farm for many years. Bill stayed right there on the farm; never left except once or twice a year he went to Rollingsford for an R&R with Jack Daniels. Then he would return to the farm, slightly worn for the wear. Bill was always part of the family even when he couldn't work any more. "Death of the Hired Man" by Robert Frost is recalled. It was like that.

There are five generations of our town in Hillside Cemetery. Harvey Johnson, the funeral director in North Berwick for many years, took care of everything when he was needed. He was much more than the funeral director; he always knew the right thing to do and in a caring way directed us.

That cemetery is the burial place for most of my aunts and uncles; the ones who loved and cared for me like their own. Some years before she died my Aunt Georgie said to me, "Betty, when they take me for my last ride to the cemetery, I want you to tell Harvey to step on it. I don't want my last ride to be a slow one. I never drove slow in my life and I don't want to go slow on my last trip." Well, when the time came, Aunt Georgie's ride was not fast. I thought about it all the way to the cemetery and I told Harvey about it, but it wasn't funny then.

To leave this tale of some sadness, there is another tale that is funny; at least I think so. My Aunt Florence and her brother Uncle Phil were looking over the big family monument in Portsmouth Cemetery. Uncle Phil was reading down all the names of the family listed with chiseled out dates of births and deaths. He noticed one missing the date of death beside it. "Look at that," he said, "they haven't put the date of death on it yet." My aunt straightened up and replied 'of course not, because that's me on there and I'm not dead yet!"

And so goes the town of North Berwick!

Banana Bread...

¼ cup shortening
1 teaspoon salt
1 cup sugar
2 eggs
1½ cups flour
1 teaspoon salt
3 bananas beaten well

Cream shortening
Add...one at a time and beat
Salt
Sugar
Eggs

Mix...
Flour
Soda
Add to the shortening mixture
Add creamed bananas

Bake in greased loaf pan at 350 degrees

This is the best banana bread I have ever had.

Maine Talk...

- We all know Mainers' talk is different from the rest of the country; and here are some old expressions and their meanings.

- Full as a tick – can't eat any more.

- High cockalorum - full of pep

- Fallen away - lost weight

- Jacked his job – quit his job

- All haired up – very excited

- Hotter than Hitty – very hot

- Spider – a large black iron frying pan

- Mackerel sky – a mottled cloudy sky that looks like the side of a mackerel

- Stuck in his craw – can't stand something

- Put the kibosh on that – squelched something

- Going gunning - going hunting
- Got a hollow leg – has a big appetite
- Nobody home upstairs – lacked brain power
- John Barleycorn – booze
- In the arms of Morpheus – sleeping
- Crazy as a coot – doesn't' make sense.
- Jawing at us – scolding us
- A cunning baby – adorable baby
- Stand of buildings – a group of farm buildings
- All the go – very popular
- Culch – household junk
- Humdinger - a real prize
- Three sheets to the wind –drunk
- Just a dite – just a little
- Going up fool's hill – a teenager doing foolish things

Household Hints from a 1930s Cookbook...

1. Cutting up hard shell squash. Use a small meat saw and cut any size wanted

2. Two tablespoons of kerosene in the boiler of white clothes will help to whiten them.

3. Salt in the oven under baking tin will prevent scorching on the bottom.

4. To get whole nuts out of the shells, soak in salt water over night. Crack on the ends.

5. When peeling onions, hold the end of a match between the lips or teeth.

6. Use olive oil for sunburn.

7. Brooms last longer if first soaked 14 minutes in strong salt water and put in the sun to dry.

8. If oven is too hot, place a basin of cold water inside the oven.

9. Cheese will keep fresh for weeks if you put a lump of sugar in the cheese dish. This will absorb moisture and prevent mildew.

10. Keep a slice of bread in the tin of brown sugar and the sugar will always be soft, never hardened.

And so we remember our times in North Berwick. From a child to a teenager to an adult, we cherished them all and the people who made them real for us.

Recipes…

Breads

Ginnie's Oatmeal Bread… 6
Swedish Tea Ring… *51*
Blueberry Pancakes… 111
Dumplings… 141
Ruth Stillings' Baking Powder Biscuits…166
Banana Bread… 222

Cookies

Spiced Cookies… 10
Annie Neal's Molasses Cookies… 20
Aggression Cookies… 70
Chocolate Crinkle Cookies… 104
Afternoon Tea Doughnuts… 133
Don't Worry's Hermits… 188
Walnut Strips… 193
Norwegian Macaroons… 198
Favorite Ginger Snaps… 201

Pies

Show Off Rhubarb Pie… *14*
Red Cinnamon Apple Pie… 163

Brambles... 180
Norwegian Apple Pie... 197
Downeast Blueberry Cobbler... 217

Pickles

Pickled Eggs... 71
Potsfield Pickles... 145
Mustard Pickles... 146

Cakes

Chocolate Cake... 44
Twenty Minute Pound Cake... 48
Cheese Cake... 130
Apple Cake... 160
Orange Sponge Cake... 172
Cherry Cake... 205

Puddings

Baked Rice Pudding... 61
Corn Pudding... 66
Grapenut Pudding... 75
Graham Cracker Pudding... 82
Yorkshire Pudding... 114
Cornflake Pudding... 154
Baked Rice Pudding... 176

Vegetables and Salads

Cranberry – Raspberry Salad… ……………*25*
Baked Beans……………………………… *26*
Molded Tomato Aspic… ………………….45
Beneath the Sea Salad… …………………58
Marion Littlefield's Baked Turnip… ……..*78*
Calico Beans… …………………………… 119
Mushroom Sandwich… …………………216

Sweets

Strawberries……………………………….31
Pink Ladies (Bars)… ……………………..32
Divinity Fudge… …………………………39
Frozen Custard…………………………….57

Meats

Swedish Meatballs… ……………………..53
Hearty Pressure Cooker Stew… …………..62
Cape Cod Pot Roast……………………….65
Oven Barbecued Spare Ribs… …………..88
Barbecued Hot Dogs………………………97
Margaret's Rigatoni… …………………… 101
Spaghetti and Meat Balls……………….127
Beef Casserole… ………………………..137
Sweet 'n' Sour Meatballs………………… 149

About The Author...

Betty Kennedy Tufts is a true "State of Mainer," born in North Berwick in 1922. She spent there, as she readily claims, a wonderful and happy childhood with her parents, grandparents, and aunts and uncles. After North Berwick High School, she graduated from Gorham, Maine State Teachers College, now the University of Southern Maine, and she became a Junior High School teacher of social studies. She taught in Maine, Pennsylvania, Massachusetts and New Hampshire.

Betty married Stan, her high school beau, who held school administrator positions in New Hampshire. With a great interest in interior decoration, they built or remodeled eight houses along the way. They retired in Wells, Maine where Betty had her own antique shop for 20 years. She also set up and sold at antique shows in New England.

They had three daughters, seven grandchildren and two great grandchildren.

A widow now, living in Wells, Maine she enjoys her family, her church, friends and mostly, the humorous side of all things.

Printed in the United States
58079LVS00001B/121-183